The Most Evil Se
of the 19'

1970s

A Decade of
Serial Killers

Jack Smith

Warning
Throughout the book, there are some descriptions of murders and crime scenes that some people might find disturbing. There might be also some language used by people involved in the murders that may not be appropriate.

Note
Words in italic are quoted words from verbatim and have been reproduced as is, including any grammatical errors and misspelled words.

ISBN: 9781081872571

Printed in the United States

MAPLEWOOD
PUBLISHING

Contents

The Deadly Decade of the 1970s

The 1970s was full of change, fast-moving trends, and explosive style. This was the decade that brought us Star Wars, mood rings, and pet rocks. But along with all of this less-than digital fun, the 1970s also brought us an awful lot of murder and mayhem.

The decade did have more than its fair share of violent crime and, amid this crime wave, were many instances of serial killers run amok. Some of the most notorious serial killers ever were active during this decade. You have, of course, the Son of Sam killings of David Berkowitz and the infamous brutality of Ted Bundy, and you also have the senseless violence of such lesser-known characters as Herbert Mullin and Edmund Kemper.

And these brutal killers didn't just terrorize their victims; they gave nightmares to folks far and wide who heard about their outrages on the nightly news. So as much as we would like to remember the 1970s as a decade of carefree fun and questionable fashion, in many ways it was a decade of dire distress. In fact, the 1970s could be considered the decade that gave birth to the concept of the serial killer as we know it today.

Sadly, this sort of mass murder has never gone away, but at least the public is a little more cognizant of the fact that such monsters lurk in our midst. This book does not seek to celebrate these purveyors of mayhem; instead, it seeks to inform law-abiding citizens of their misdeeds in order to remind us that the world can be a dangerous place. Because knowledge, after all, is power.

And if the motivation of serial killers can be boiled down to just one thing, it would be that all these criminals are seeking to empower themselves by terrifying others. But if we take the time to examine just how these monstrosities cloaked in human skin operate, we just might find that the power of fear that these miscreants attempt to wield over their unsuspecting human brethren will rather quickly disappear.

***

In many ways, the 1970s was the decade that crystalized the concept of the serial killer. Those days of disco past were also the heyday of some of the most notorious serial killers of all time. This book explores some of the best documented of these cases—and some of the most shocking, horrific and downright bizarre. This book does not seek to glorify crime, but it does stand as a testament and a warning about the darker side of human nature.

The Grisly Craft of Randy Kraft

Randy Kraft was the youngest child of Opal and Harold Craft, born on March 19, 1945, at the tail end of World War II. Although the family was of modest means, both parents were industrious, hard workers who always provided for their children. Randy seemed to be a well-adjusted child, and by the time he was in high school, he was a straight-A student with a burgeoning social life.

He had lots of friends and a few girlfriends—even though many speculated that he might be gay. Kraft would later acknowledge that he had already realized his true sexual orientation during this period, but as homosexuality was not socially acceptable in the early 1960s, he kept his inclinations a closely guarded secret.

Kraft graduated from high school on June 13, 1963, and soon enrolled at Claremont Men's College (now Claremont McKenna College). Here he finally embraced his hidden sexual identity and began to openly date men. He also shed his previously conservative leanings, became an active member of the Democratic Party, and supported the campaign of Robert Kennedy in 1968. That was also the year he received his bachelor's degree and joined the Air Force. He served with distinction before being discharged after revealing his sexual orientation. He told his parents that he was gay at around the same time; his father was highly upset, while his mother was much more sympathetic but still "disappointed".

Kraft got a job as a bartender, and eventually his own apartment. Initially, he stuck to himself and stayed off the radar. But he came to the attention of authorities in March of 1970 after befriending a 13-year-old boy named Joey Fancher. Presenting himself as a mentor who wanted to help, Kraft told Joey that he could stay at his apartment. Soon enough, the real reasons for the invitation became clear when he drugged and sexually assaulted the teenager.

The next day, after Kraft left for work, Joey fled the apartment and asked a passerby to summon an ambulance. He was taken to the hospital, where he had his stomach pumped to remove the drugs, and was then interviewed by police. He confided that he had been beaten and drugged, but he declined to mention that he had been sexually assaulted. As the youth admitted to taking the drugs voluntarily, and a subsequent search of Kraft's apartment turned up nothing untoward, Kraft was ultimately not prosecuted in the case.

Kraft's murder spree began the following year and spanned from 1971 to 1983, leaving as many as 67 dead. The victims were all males between the ages of 13 and 35. Kraft typically accosted them in public places and got them into his vehicle under the pretense of giving them a ride somewhere before plying them with a combination of drugs and alcohol in order to render them compliant before he sexually assaulted them. This was followed by death through strangulation, a savage beating, or a combination of both. Kraft would then dump the bodies along remote stretches of highway all throughout Southern California (and sometimes as far afield as Michigan). It was this fact that would earn him the nickname of the "Freeway Killer".

His first victim was a 30-year-old man named Wayne Kukette who was a regular at a gay nightclub called The Stable. Wayne was found dead on the Ortega Highway on October 5, 1971. The next victim was a young man named Edward Moore, who was a Marine stationed at Camp Pendleton. He had last been seen on the base before his dead body turned up on December 26, 1972. The corpse was badly banged up, and upon examination, it was clear it had been thrown from a car traveling at a high rate of speed down the highway.

Just a few weeks later, another victim—who would never be identified—turned up on another lonely stretch of highway in a very similar condition. The police was shocked at what was happening, and even more so when another victim was found near Huntington Beach just a couple of months later. Kevin Bailey, 17, had met a particularly cruel end, having been castrated and sodomized before he was finally put to death. Two more victims emerged shortly thereafter. They had been strangled and discarded on the side of the road like all the rest.

By the time 1975 rolled around, the killer had racked up several more victims on what would later be referred to as his scorecard—for Kraft was indeed keeping score of those he had killed throughout the 1970s, as was discovered upon his eventual arrest. The death toll had now reached a point where police finally had to admit that they had a true-blue serial killer on their hands. They began to create an in-depth profile of the murderer who was lurking the highways and byways of Southern California. But the killings continued, and they still had no real lead as to who was committing them and why he was killing in such prolific fashion.

It wasn't until the slaying of Keith Crotwell that spring that the cold trail left by the killer began to heat up. Kraft had supplied the young man with Valium and alcohol before assaulting and ultimately killing him; his skull was found a few months later at a Long Beach marina.

Shortly before Keith's disappearance, patrons of a local gay bar had seen him slumped over in the passenger seat of a Ford Mustang. Upon hearing of his death, these regulars took it upon themselves to search for the Mustang. When they found it in a nearby neighborhood, they discreetly copied down the license plate number and turned it over to police.

This led to a police interview for Kraft on May 19th. At first, he repeatedly denied ever knowing Keith Crotwell. But by the second round of questioning, he had concocted an alibi that he believed would put him in the clear. He admitted to knowing Keith but claimed that after an evening of drugs and alcohol he had driven Keith to an isolated locale where his car had become stuck in an embankment. Leaving Keith by himself, Kraft had walked off in search of a gas station payphone where he could summon help. Upon his return, however, Keith was nowhere to be seen.

Even though Kraft's roommate backed up this claim by testifying that Kraft had indeed placed a phone call to him reporting that his car was stuck on the side of the road, police were immediately skeptical of the story. They wanted to file a case against Kraft, but after the coroner reported that Keith had most likely died from accidental drowning, their case fell apart and they had no choice but to let him go.

Possibly perturbed by his brush with the law, Kraft lay low until the very last day of the year. On December 31, 1975, he took a 22-year-old man named Mark Hall to an isolated desert canyon and proceeded to unleash all of his pent-up fury onto the suffering form of his unfortunate victim. In what became known as the cruelest and most sadistic of all of Kraft's killings, Mark was tied to a tree, tortured with cigarette burns and cuts inflicted alternately from Kraft's cigarette lighter and a broken bottle, and ultimately had his penis cut off and shoved into his own anus. Horribly enough, the autopsy revealed that much of this torment had occurred while he was alive and fully conscious.

Kraft continued his reign of terror through the rest of the 1970s and on into the early 1980s. His rampage of death and destruction would not end until the early morning hours of May 14, 1983, when he was pulled over by police after a night of binge drinking and mayhem. As Kraft stumbled out of his car to meet the patrolmen on that isolated stretch of road, it was obvious that he had been driving drunk. But when the officers noticed a man slumped over in the passenger seat of the car, they knew that there was more to the story. One of them approached the man and tried to get his attention, but he didn't move. The officer tried to shake him awake—and realized that he was cold to the touch. He felt for a pulse and discovered that the man was most certainly dead—and not from alcohol poisoning. The man had clear ligature marks on his neck, indicating that he had been strangled. Closer examination showed that his hands were bound together by a shoelace. The victim was later found to be a 25-year-old soldier named Terry Lee Gambrel.

Kraft was taken into custody and the car was examined. Several blood stains were found on the carpeting—and when the carpet was taken out for analysis, an envelope with macabre photos of the Freeway Killer's previous victims was discovered underneath. The fact that Kraft had photos of so many young men who were missing and presumed dead was damning enough—but not as damning as the binder found in the vehicle's trunk. The binder contained a piece of paper with names and notations of all the victims.

Still, authorities were meticulous in assembling the evidence against Kraft, and his trial did not commence until September 26, 1988. After mounting a vigorous defense, Kraft was ultimately found guilty and sentenced to death—but thanks to the backlog on California's death row, as of 2019, he is still waiting in the queue for justice to be served.

Ted Bundy
Burn Bundy, Burn!

If any serial killer's name screams out at us from the 1970s, it's the name of Ted Bundy. His birth name was actually Theodore Robert Cowell, and he was born to a young, unwed mother named Elanor Louise Cowell in 1946. Giving birth out of wedlock was a social taboo at the time, and so the Cowell family quietly placed their daughter into a "maternity home" so that she could go through her pregnancy away from prying eyes. Once the baby was born, Elanor's parents passed it off as their own, thereby saving their daughter from certain disgrace.

In some ways, this was a noble effort to protect their daughter from the life of a social pariah. But even if it was a white lie, it was a lie, and a very confused Ted Bundy grew up believing that his mother was his sister and his grandmother and grandfather were his parents. His mother-turned-sister eventually married a man named Johnnie Culpepper Bundy, thereby giving her son a new last name and—so she hoped—a new lease on a happy and drama-free life.

At first, her plans seemed to be working. Under her guidance Ted grew into an academically gifted student, graduating from high school with honors and going on to attend classes at the University of Puget Sound. But Bundy felt inadequate around the mostly affluent students who attended this school and soon transferred to the more accessible University of Washington.

It was here that Bundy met the woman who would become the love of his life: Stephanie Brooks. The two shared a passion for skiing, among other things, and were soon an inseparable pair on the slopes. But what to Stephanie was more or less just a fling meant so much more to Bundy. She was a couple of years older than him, and she taught him a lot about both life and love. Unfortunately for Bundy's fragile psyche, she also taught him a hard lesson in heartache. Because shortly after Stephanie graduated from the University of Washington, she broke off her relationship with Bundy and moved to California to pursue her career.

Back in Washington without Stephanie, Bundy was an emotional wreck. Too depressed to attend class, he decided to take time off from the university and travel back to his birthplace in Pennsylvania to explore the questions about his upbringing that had haunted him his entire life. When he found his original birth certificate, it confirmed the long-standing rumor that the woman who had pretended to be his big sister was actually his mom. He also discovered that his dad was an Air Force veteran referred to as Lord Marshal, but nothing else about him. With his father a mystery, Bundy felt that his own identity was also a complete mystery, and when he finally returned to Washington to go back to school, he had more questions than answers.

He was still obsessed with his ex-girlfriend Stephanie, and on one occasion he even thumbed his way to her workplace in California. When a thoroughly disheveled Ted Bundy clumsily confronted his former lover face to face, Stephanie tried to let him down easy, but she made it abundantly clear that her decision to leave him was final. Completely devastated, Bundy at first seemed to lose all desire to go on with his life.

But in the fall of 1969, he managed to do an about-face, pick himself up, and return to his studies at the University of Washington. Suddenly full of determination to succeed, Bundy became a model student, earning a 4.0 GPA. He was on the fast track for success and set his sights on attending law school as soon as he obtained his bachelor's.

An ironic footnote in Bundy's life is that he helped finance his college tuition by working at—of all places—a suicide hotline. Here, as Bundy author and former acquaintance Anne Rule once described it, the same Bundy who "took lives" also "saved lives" as an outreach counselor. Bundy was reportedly very good at his work and was one of the most celebrated members of the crisis center's team.

Bundy graduated in 1972 and was slated to attend the University of Utah Law School in 1973. After he landed a highly paid position with the Washington State Republican Party, though, he changed gears and enrolled at the University of Puget Sound Law School instead.

He also decided the time was ripe to reach out to his old flame Stephanie, and he was right. She was impressed with how far Bundy had come, and after a few dates, she fell into his orbit once again. But his desire to have Stephanie back had been trumped by an even greater desire for vengeance. Bundy's cunning, conniving mind went to work, and just as soon as he had Stephanie buttered up and ready to declare her undying love for him, he cut her off. He suddenly made himself scarce and ignored all of her phone calls. When she finally got a hold of him and asked why he had suddenly cast her to the side, he delivered the flat-response "I have no idea what you mean" before hanging up on her.

After he killed his relationship with Stephanie, Bundy began his real killing. He took his first life in 1974, in between classes at law school, when he broke into the residence of a young college student named Karen Sparks. Bundy sneaked up on the sleeping girl, quietly pulled a metal bedpost out of her bed, and then repeatedly bludgeoned her with it. After beating her unconscious, he inserted the end of the bedpost into her vagina. But beyond all odds, this first Bundy victim survived. She had severe brain and internal injuries and she was permanently disfigured, but she did not die.

Bundy's next victim was not so lucky. Soon afterward, he broke into another campus residence and caught young Lynda Ann Healy completely unaware. Adding kidnapping to his repertoire, he ripped her from her own home so that he could systematically brutalize her later. He ended up beating the poor girl to death and ditching her body. Bundy then repeated nearly the same sadistic acts on a girl named Donna Gail Manson, whom he dispatched in very similar fashion on March 12, 1974.

When investigators found Donna's savaged body, they began to suspect that they were looking at a habitual offender, and this was all but proven when young Susan Elaine turned up dead shortly thereafter. Susan's death also produced witnesses who were able to describe a potential perpetrator and modus operandi: There were several reports of a man with "his arm in a sling" who was going around asking women to help him carry his textbooks. The man was nice enough—indeed, he was handsome and charming—but to some, he seemed just a bit too inviting. And they were absolutely correct. Bundy was pretending to have a broken arm to win sympathy and cause his victims to let their guard down. Making himself appear as harmless as possible, he would lure the girls to his car, parked far out of sight. Then, after they helped him put his books inside, he would strike, forcing them into the car with him.

After several girls turned up dead after helping this mysterious stranger during the summer of 1974, police knew for certain that there was a serial killer in their midst. And after park-goers in Washington had a direct encounter with that killer in July, they also had a name. When a young lady named Janice Ott disappeared after "assisting" Bundy, several eyewitnesses reported a man with his arm in a cast, chatting up pretty young girls. What's more, some of them distinctly remembered the man saying that his name was Ted. So now authorities had their first profile of the killer: a younger man named Ted, who was handsome, charming, intelligent, and pretending to have a broken arm. And a few of the witnesses had also seen the guy's car, a Volkswagen Beetle. The killer now had a name, a car, and with the help of police sketch artists, a composite likeness to post all over the whole tri-state area.

Bundy knew that his days were numbered—numbered, as it turned out, all the way up to August 16, 1975, when a policeman named Bob Hayward was on the beat in a residential community and noticed Bundy's Volkswagen Beetle drive-through. Not recognizing the car from the neighborhood, the officer turned on his spotlight to read its license plate. While police had the vehicle's description, they didn't have its plate number, so Bundy might have escaped even then if he had kept his cool. But he had been increasingly edgy of late, and the sight of a police car shining a spotlight on him was enough to make him lose it. He cut his headlights, hit the gas, and took off. This, of course, was all the reason Hayward needed to switch on his red and blue lights and launch after the strange car. The high-speed chase that followed lasted for several miles as Bundy blew through intersection after intersection. Eventually, though, realizing that he could not get away from the doggedly pursing Hayward, he gave up and pulled into a service station.

To the amazement of the officer who had been chasing him for several nail-biting minutes, Bundy then hopped out of his car and dumbly announced, "Well, I guess I'm lost." Considering how many of these high-speed chases turn into fatal shootings, and considering that Hayward kept his gun trained on Bundy at all times as he ordered him to give him his license and registration, Bundy was lucky he wasn't shot on the spot. Upon being questioned about what he was doing lurking around the neighborhood in the wee hours in the morning, Bundy told the officer that he had caught a late-night showing of *The Towering Inferno* at the local drive-in and "became lost" on his way back. There was just one problem with this story: That theater was not currently showing that particular film—and Hayward knew it. Shining his flashlight into Bundy's car, the officer then took note of the following incriminating items: a ski mask, a crowbar, an ice pick, and a length of rope. He wasn't sure if Bundy was planning a break-in or what, but he knew he had enough to take him down to the station for further questioning, so he cuffed him and proceeded to do just that.

Bundy apparently calmed himself down on the ride there, because he remained cool as a cucumber when the detectives started to interrogate him. The ski mask, he insisted, was for skiing, and all the other items were simple, everyday stuff that just about any motorist would have. And while it was certainly a stretch to say that most motorists have ice picks and crowbars lying around in their back seats, there was no real evidence that Bundy had committed a crime. He was let go.

Even so, he remained a clear suspect, and the police were actively waiting and watching for any further indications of malfeasance on his part. They had their suspicions confirmed when a witness who had identified Bundy in a previous police lineup came forward. Her name was Carol DaRonch, and in late 1974 she had had a frightening encounter with a man matching Bundy's description. The man told her that he was an undercover cop and that someone had vandalized her car in the parking lot. He then asked her to ride with him down to headquarters so she could fill out a report on the supposed incident. It soon became clear, however, that he was no undercover officer. Despite her protests, he drove her to a remote area and then tried to handcuff her. Carol was a fighter, though, and she unleashed more resistance than Bundy was used to dealing with. He managed to cuff one of her hands, but she was able to keep him from slapping a cuff on the other one. With only one cuff in place, Carol fought her way out of Bundy's vehicle and fled on foot. Bundy panicked and drove off while Carol flagged down a passing motorist who came to her aid.

Due to Carol's testimony and positive ID in the lineup, Bundy was re-arrested and brought to trial in the spring of 1976. It wasn't a murder trial, but a solid case had been developed against him for assault and kidnapping. Bundy was ultimately found guilty and given the rather wide-ranging sentence of 1 to 15 years. But even if Bundy was out in a year, detectives were amassing enough evidence to link him to further, much more heinous crimes. A new trial was accordingly scheduled for 1977.

Bundy, realizing that the jig was up, managed to make a daring escape by jumping out of a courthouse window. The escape was short-lived, however, as he was recaptured several days later. He was set to stand trial again in early January of 1978, but unbelievably, Ted Bundy escaped once more before this trial date arrived. And this time he was not immediately caught.

After hitchhiking, riding a bus, flying on an airplane, and traveling by train, he wound up in Tallahassee, Florida, where he used the money he had saved up while in prison to rent an apartment near Florida State University. He tried to lie low at first, but it wasn't long before he once again succumbed to his urge to kill. In the grip of this sick impulse, he slaughtered an FSU coed named Margaret Bowman in early 1978. Taking all of his anger out on this innocent young woman, he broke into her home and savagely beat her before throttling her to death. Like a true maniac, Bundy then went to the nearby room in which Margaret's housemate Lisa Levy was sleeping and beat her into unconsciousness. He also bit her, almost tearing away one of her nipples with his teeth. After Bundy fled the scene, Lisa died as she was being rushed to the emergency room.

15

Bundy was on a real rampage that night, and after slipping away from Margaret and Lisa's home, he busted into another campus dwelling where he attacked Kathy Kleiner and Karen Chandler. Bundy gave both girls a savage beating, then ran to a nearby university apartment where he found a girl named Chary Thomas. Catching Chary off guard, he waylaid her and left her with a fractured skull and broken jaw.

After visiting this unprecedented mayhem on the previously peaceful FSU campus, Bundy decided to hide out for a while. But he couldn't stop killing for long, and on February 8th he stole a van and began to drive around Florida looking for a new victim. It was in this fashion that he seized the girl who would be his last victim, 12 year-old Kimberly Leach. After brutalizing this poor girl, Bundy ditched her body in the Suwanee River.

Shortly after this horrid crime he was pulled over and apprehended. After years of subterfuge and running from the law, Bundy was finally made to answer for his crimes. He was tried, convicted on all counts, and given a death sentence. However, Bundy would sit on death row for another decade before he was finally put to death in the electric chair on January 24, 1989.

In the ten years following his 1979 sentencing, the public had developed quite a thirst to see justice meted out to this killer, as was apparent in the eager anticipation of the crowds of people that gathered around the prison where Bundy was being executed. Cheering on the execution process, these onlookers chanted, "Burn, Bundy, burn!" In the midst of this circus-like backdrop, thousands of volts were sent through Bundy's body, reducing him to a lifeless corpse in a matter of seconds. Finally, as they say, justice was served. But no matter how many volts they unleashed on Ted Bundy that day, none of it will ever bring back the lives that he destroyed.

Herbert Mullin
The Homicidal Defender of the Earth

Killers can be divided into several different categories based on a variety of factors. There are lust killers who kill to satiate their own warped sexual impulses; there are revenge killers seeking to balance the scales through murder; and for lack of a better explanation, there are killers who just seem to like to kill. But serial killer Herbert Mullin does not easily fit into any of these categories. For him, killing was part of a bizarre mission to save the planet.

Yes, you heard right. Mullin believed that he had to sacrifice a few lives to spare all of humanity. If you think that sounds the slightest bit strange, then you are beginning to understand why Mullin belongs in a category all his own. And no, he wasn't some ecoterrorist worried about overpopulation—Mullin was so out of his mind and delusional that he believed he had been handpicked to kill random people all over California to prevent earthquakes.

The severity of his mental illness was made clear when he attempted to describe a little something called "The Die Song" to one of his many psychiatrists—but you hardly need to be a shrink to listen to his words and decide that this man was completely off his rocker: "You see, the thing is, people get together, say, in the White House. People like to sing the die song, you know, people like to sing the die song. I am president of my class when I graduate from High School, [I] can tell two, possibly three male *Homo sapiens* to die. I can sing that song to them and they'll have to kill themselves or be killed—an automobile accident, a knifing, a gunshot wound. You ask me why this is? And I say, well they have to do that to protect the ground from an earthquake, because all of the other people in the community had been dying all year long, and my class, we have to chip in so to speak to the darkness, we have to die also. And people would rather sing the die song than murder."

Herbert Mullin was a California native who came into this world on April 18, 1947. He had a good but stern upbringing and generally did well both academically and socially in high school. He was even voted "Most Likely to Succeed" in his class.

And then one traumatic event sent him over the deep end. His best friend Dean, a buddy in whom Mullin confided all of his innermost desires and fears, died in a car accident. This was the first time that Mullin had ever faced an irrevocable loss of a loved one, and it overwhelmed him. In a state of shock, he began to obsess about Dean's demise and even built a small shrine to him in his bedroom. His now-chaotic mind would fixate on this shrine as he mediated on all the uncertainties that had invaded his life.

Over the next few years, Mullin gradually withdrew from his former social groups as his mental state continued to deteriorate. He was 21 years old and still living at home when his break with reality finally became clear enough to inspire his relatives to get him some help. The family had all gathered at the table to celebrate his parents' 29th wedding anniversary. Mullin appeared to be in a strange state from the beginning, and he had a peculiar focus on the husband of his visiting sister. Inexplicably and to the bewilderment of everyone present, he began to repeat everything that his brother-in-law did. If the guy said "Pass the potatoes", Mullin would pipe in with "Pass the potatoes!" If he cleared his throat, Mullin would clear his throat also. Initially, this passed as offbeat humor, but when it continued unabated over the course of an hour with no punch line in sight it became downright strange—and a clear sign that something was seriously wrong.

After this episode, Mullin was persuaded to go to the hospital to get checked out. A psychiatrist evaluated him and quickly surmised that he was in the throes of schizophrenia. The attending clinician documented that Mullin's prognosis was poor, but didn't offer much in the way of help or advice to him or his family. And since Mullin was an adult who seemed to pose no threat of violence, even though it was certain that he was severely troubled, he was discharged—put back on the street to become yet another mental health patient that the system had conveniently washed its hands of.

Not having received any meaningful treatment for his condition, Mullin began to bounce around from place to place and job to job, never staying in either one for very long. He worked as a trucker, a stocker, a dish washer at a restaurant, and a clerk at a gas station, but no matter what he did he couldn't shake the voices that he heard in his own head. The voices came on as mostly indistinct murmurings at first, but as the years went by they crystallized into clear words—and then urgent commands. And none of the commands that issued from Mullin's mind were of the benevolent kind. They usually ordered him to hurt or humiliate himself in some fashion, such as repeatedly burning himself with cigarettes.

It was in this bewildered state that Mullin returned to his parents' home in 1972 at the age of 25. He soon became obsessed with the idea that California was going to be rocked by a catastrophic earthquake, apparently because his birthday of April 18th was the anniversary of the great 1906 San Francisco earthquake that had devastated the city at the beginning of the 20th century. As schizophrenic patients often do, Mullin took this random coincidence and made it into a direct connection, giving his life the perceived purpose of stopping the next big quake.

And how was Herbert Mullin going to stop the next big quake? By killing people, of course! It is next to impossible for a sane, rational person to understand how someone could come to such a bizarre conclusion, but Mullin felt that the very Earth was crying out for blood, and that if he killed enough people, he could satiate the ground's bloodlust. And so it was that Mullin took to the street to obey the disembodied voices he heard, hunting for a victim for his human sacrifice.

The first victim he found was a vagrant named Lawrence White who was hitchhiking along the highway. Feigning car trouble, Mullin pulled over, popped his hood, and pretended to examine the engine. Striking up a conversation with White, he then asked him to take a look—and as soon as White's back was turned to perform this good deed, Mullin began savagely beating him to death.

Mullin later claimed that this homeless drifter had "sent him a telepathic message" stating that he was the biblical prophet Jonah and wished to be killed so that he could "save others". He also claimed to hear other telepathic messages from time to time, for example that his "parents had deliberately tried to ruin his life by sending telepathic messages to his schoolmates, threatening to kill them in the afterlife if they played with him." It's common enough for young people to blame their parents for all kinds of things, but claiming that they were threatening to kill your friends "in the afterlife" is certainly taking the blame game quite a few steps further!

At any rate, shortly after this brutal crime, Mullin picked up another hitchhiker, this one a 24-year-old university student named Mary Guilfoyle. After gaining her confidence and getting her into his vehicle, Mullin ruthlessly stabbed and slashed Mary until she died. Both of these slayings occurred in October of 1972.

Whatever remained of Mullin's rational mind must have felt pretty guilty about what had happened, because the following month he took himself to a Catholic church to confess his sins. It's not clear exactly what the priest on the other side of the confessional box said to him, but when Mullin somehow got the idea that the man had just assented to becoming the next sacrificial victim to stave off earthquakes, all bets were off. Following this insane notion, Mullin proceeded to beat and stab the priest—Father Henri Tomei—to death. A parishioner noticed Mullin's rapid departure and reported a tall, thin youth, in "dark clothing and black boots" fleeing the church, and a murder investigation was duly launched. However, the slaying of Father Henri was not yet linked to the hitchhiker killings, which were still believed to be random, isolated incidents.

While the authorities were trying to piece things together, Mullin tried to change course and become a U.S. Marine. For someone as crazy as Mullin, this actually made a surprising amount of sense: If he really *had* been appointed to kill people as a sacrifice to prevent an earthquake, fighting on the front lines of the Vietnam War would have been a convenient—not to mention legal—way of doing so. Mullin passed both the physical and (despite his obvious delusions) mental assessments with ease and was quickly slated for deployment. But then the routine police background check came back with a long list of arrests that Mullin had accumulated through the years. These were all for minor issues such as disturbing the peace, but they were enough to make the recruiting sergeant raise his eyebrows and shelve the enlistment.

Mullin was enraged at this rejection, considering it part of a larger conspiracy to sabotage his mission, but he didn't let it dissuade him. Unable to kill any Vietnamese, he went back to targeting people in his immediate vicinity. For his next victim, he decided to kill an old high school friend of his named Jim Gianera. It turned out that Jim had moved in the meantime, and as he was searching for his new residence Mullin ran into a mutual friend of theirs, a woman named Kathy Francis. Kathy happily gave Mullin Jim's new address, and Mullin promptly drove over and shot both him and his wife execution-style before butchering their corpses with a knife. He then went back to Kathy's house to thank her for her help in tracking down Jim, expressing his gratitude in the only way he knew how—by killing her and her two children.

Mullin's murder spree continued a few months later when he stumbled across the campsite of four young kids in February of 1973. Pretending to be park ranger, Mullin ordered them to leave the campground, but the youngsters refused. Whether as a retort to their insolence or as a sacrifice to the dark forces causing California's earthquakes, Mullin shot them all dead on the spot.

Just a few days later he was cruising a nearby neighborhood and decided to pick off the man who would be his last victim. Californian retiree Fred Perez was simply out doing some yard work when he caught Mullin's eye. Mullin casually turned his car around and put it in park before hopping out and firing his gun. A lone bullet sliced through Fred's heart, and an emotionless Mullin got back inside his car and slowly cruised out of the neighborhood—slowly enough that multiple neighbors got his plate number. Police were not far behind, and in a matter of mere minutes Mullin was pulled over and arrested without incident.

Mullin readily confessed to the murders and explained in depth the bizarre notion that he was killing people to stave off a massive earthquake. And strangely enough, just a few days after Mullin was arrested, California was hit with a 5.8 magnitude earthquake—whereas all the time he had been killing, there had been none. Authorities, however, wrote this off as a coincidence and charged the man with ten counts of murder. He stood trial on July 30, 1973, not to prove that he had killed (he admitted that) but to determine whether he was of sound enough mind to be punished for the killings.

Mullin's defense team, naturally, brought up his history of mental illness and argued that he was innocent by reason of insanity. His ramblings most certainly did make him appear unhinged, but the prosecution used the fact that he had returned to kill Kathy after murdering his friend Jim to show a degree of premeditation. According to this theory, it wasn't uncontrollable, insane rage that guided Mullin; it was calculated, premeditated homicide plain and simple. This seemed to sway the jury, and Herbert Mullin was found guilty of murder on August 19, 1973, and sentenced to life at California's Mule Creek State Prison, where he still sits to this very day.

When Edmund Kemper Lost His Temper

Edmund Kemper was one of the most notorious serial killers of the 1970s, mostly due to the sheer senselessness of his acts. Kemper wasn't always a killer, of course; just like the rest of us, he came into this world as an innocent baby when he was born on December 18, 1948. His father and grandfather were also named Edmund Kemper, making this future serial killer's full name Edmund Kemper III. His mother, Clarnell, sought to make a good life for their family after her husband returned from fighting in World War II.

Edmund was a very intelligent child, but he also had a cruel streak that emerged fairly early on. He displayed this cruelty on family pets; on one occasion, for example, a 10-year-old Edmund decided it would be fun to bury his cat alive. (Fun for him, that is, not the cat.) With the animal howling and screaming, Edmund mercilessly shoveled dirt over it and waited for it to perish. When he was sure it was dead, he dug it up, chopped its head off, and put it up on a stick. It was as if he was a medieval king punishing a traitor—but whatever crimes he was punishing the poor feline *for* obviously existed only in young Edmund's warped mind.

And Edmund didn't just want to punish others; often enough, he wanted to punish *himself*. A favorite childhood game of his, in fact, was one that he and his sisters called "the electric chair". In this twisted foray into imagination, Edmund would sit in a chair and have one of his sisters flip an imaginary switch, then pretend to be electrocuted as he writhed and tossed himself around as if in the throes of a lethal current.

As decidedly odd as little Edmund was already, he got much worse after his parents' 1957 divorce. His domineering and emotionally abusive mother constantly badgered him with verbal disparagement. Kemper was a big kid, growing to over six feet tall and weighing around 300 pounds by the time he was 15 years old, and Clarnell gave him grief about this just as much as she did about what she termed his "weirdo personality". She apparently thought that her hulking giant of a son was *so* weird that she would lock the basement where he slept as if she were afraid of what he might do to her and his sisters if he were to wake up in the middle of the night and venture out of his subterranean lair.

At some point, however, the teenage Edmund Kemper III escaped his mother's watchful and unkind scrutiny long enough to embark upon a search for his father. He tracked him down to his house in Van Nuys, California. Edmund Kemper II, who had remarried and gained a stepson, was obviously both surprised and ill-prepared for this sudden intrusion. Nevertheless, he allowed his son to stay with him until he could make arrangements for his parents to take him in. Kemper's paternal grandmother and grandfather lived on a remote ranch in the North Fork Mountains. They were kind and considerate enough to take their grandson in—and they would end up paying for this kindness with their lives.

Because it was indeed Kemper's own grandparents who became his first (human) murder victims. The incident occurred on August 27, 1964, on an evening when young Kemper was alone with his grandmother. They were seated at the kitchen table when they got into a heated argument. The details of their disagreement are unclear, but apparently it was bad enough to cause Kemper to storm off to the back of the house, grab his grandfather's hunting rifle, and return to use his grandmother for target practice. He shot her in the head, and then, as her body twisted and contorted in its death throes, he shot her a couple more times through the back for good measure.

A short time later, Kemper's grandfather came home, carrying a bag of groceries, and Kemper shot him on sight. Kemper later claimed that this was actually a "mercy killing" so that his grandfather wouldn't have to go through the sorrow of seeing his murdered wife. As to why he shot his grandmother in the first place, Kemper simply stated that he "just wanted to see what it felt like to kill Grandma."

After the shootings, Kemper called the police himself and did not resist arrest. He was soon evaluated by a psychiatrist, who diagnosed the 15-year-old as a paranoid schizophrenic, and then interned at the Atascadero State Hospital in a wing reserved for the criminally insane. However, most of the therapists who examined Kemper at the hospital vehemently disagreed with the diagnosis of schizophrenia. They reported that Kemper did not demonstrate the classic symptoms of wild flights of ideas, hallucinations, delusions, and bizarre thinking. Instead they gave him a broader classification of "personality trait disturbance, passive aggressive type."

Kemper quickly learned how to ingratiate himself with his caretakers, who soon viewed him as a "model patient" and allowed him great freedom in the ward. He would later admit that he was simply trying to manipulate the hospital staff to his own ends—and it worked. Due to his "good behavior", Kemper was released just a few years after the brutal slaying of his grandparents, on the very day he turned 21—December 18, 1969.

With nowhere else to go, Kemper was sent to live with his hated mother. Clarnell had since remarried and started a new life in Aptos, where she worked at the nearby campus of the University of California Santa Cruz. Kemper did quite well with the new arrangements, and after a psychiatric hearing on November 29, 1972, it was determined that his criminal record would be thrown out since he "posed no threat to society".

Or as his probation psychiatrist stated at the time, "If I were to see this patient without having any history available or getting any history from him, I would think that we're dealing with a very well-adjusted young man who had initiative, intelligence and who was free of any psychiatric illnesses. It is my opinion that he has made a very excellent response to the years of treatment and rehabilitation and I would see no psychiatric reason to consider him to be of any danger to himself or to any member of society. [And therefore] I would consider it reasonable to have a permanent expunction of his juvenile records."

With a clean slate behind him, Kemper seemed to be earnestly trying to turn over a new leaf. He began to attend community college and for a time even looked into joining the police force. However, he was ultimately rejected—not because of the heavy personal baggage of having killed his grandparents (legally, that had been expunged) but because of his large size (he was nearly seven feet tall). Nevertheless, Kemper remained friendly with the officers he had met and often frequented a local police hangout called the "Jury Room" where he would drink and hobnob with off-duty officers who later remembered him as a "gentle giant".

At the same time, though, his relationship with his mother was deteriorating along familiar lines, with the two of them falling into almost constant bickering. According to Kemper the blame for these arguments lay mostly on Clarnell, who would start knock-down, drag-out fights over something as trivial as brushing his teeth. Unable to live with such an overbearing tyrant, Kemper saved up his money and moved in with a friend as soon as possible.

He got a job with the California Highway Department, started dating a young woman who would qualify as his first girlfriend, and bought a motorcycle. While riding it one day he was struck by a car. He won $15,000 in a subsequent civil suit and used the money to purchase a 1969 Ford Galaxie—the same model notoriously used by another 1970s serial killer, David "Son of Sam" Berkowitz.

In this vehicle Kemper took to cruising around ogling all the women walking up and down the heavily trafficked California strip. He was surprised by the number of female hitchhikers, and he began to pick them up. At first, he was a perfect gentleman to these women, driving them to their destinations without incident. But eventually he began to experience homicidal urges—and to carry around plastic bags that were essentially murder kits loaded with knives and handcuffs.

The summer of 1972 saw the first of what would become a string of murders adding up to eight victims—including Kemper's own mother. The first two were a couple of college students, Anita Mary Luchessa and Mary Ann Pesce. Kemper picked them up promising to give them a ride back to the campus of Stanford University. Instead, he drove them to a secluded area where he stabbed and strangled them to death. He later said that he had intended to rape them but found himself too "embarrassed" to do so; when he was handcuffing one of the terrified women and accidentally "brushed the back of [his] hand against one of her breasts" he immediately apologized, nervously remarking, "Whoops, I'm sorry". Thinking on his feet, Kemper recovered from this faux pas by slaughtering the pair. He then hauled them back to his apartment, where he finally worked up the nerve to "desecrate" their cold, unfeeling corpses. After he had his fill of

29

fooling around with the dead bodies, he chopped them up and discarded them piecemeal, tied up in plastic bags that he left scattered on the slopes of the nearby Loma Prieta mountain.

His next victim was a 15-year-old girl named Aiko Koo. Young Aiko was a dance student who had just missed the bus to her recital. Desperate to get there on time, she flagged down Kemper, who just happened to be driving by and gladly offered to give her a ride. But following his already-established MO, instead of taking Aiko to her dance recital, he drove her out to the middle of nowhere with the intention of killing her. He was still no expert at this sort of thing, though, and he actually managed to lock himself out of the car, with Aiko inside, as he prepared to do the nefarious deed. Unfortunately, Aiko did not take the opportunity to escape; when the annoyed Kemper ordered her to unlock the car and let him back in, she meekly complied. Seconds later he was strangling her unconscious. He then assaulted her comatose body before killing her and stuffing her into his trunk. After stopping at a local bar to have a drink and relish his misdeeds, he brought Aiko's body to his apartment to defile it further. When he was finally finished, he cut the corpse into pieces, bagged them, and dumped the bags just as he had done before.

In early 1973 Kemper left his apartment to move back in with his argumentative mother. Around this time he picked up another young woman, Cynthia Schall, drove her to a remote area, and murdered her by way of his .22-caliber pistol. Astonishingly, he then smuggled the body into his mother's house and stuffed it into his bedroom closet. When Clarnell went to work, he pulled out the corpse, assaulted it, and took it apart like all the rest. Most of the parts he again discarded in remote locations, but the head he buried in his mother's own garden. That February, Kemper picked up two more college students, Rosalind Heather Thorpe and Alice Helen Liu. As before, he drove them to a remote area before shooting them execution-style, and once again he took the corpses back home, desecrated and dismembered them, and tossed the severed parts.

On April 20, 1973, Kemper ambushed his own mother and beat her to death with a hammer. His brutality apparently knew no familial bounds, because he proceeded to commit his typical acts of depravity upon her corpse. He then took her apart, as he did all his victims—but he had a special fixation on Clarnell's tongue and vocal cords, since he had spent so many years being screamed at by these speech organs. He removed both of them and shoved them down the garbage disposal, but they were too tough for the device to handle and shot right back out, smacking him in the face. He figured that this was probably "appropriate" considering how much Clarnell had "bitched and screamed" at him over the years; it seemed fitting that her nagging tongue, which had ridiculed and mocked him his whole life, would come back to smack him in the face.

Shortly afterward Kemper decided to take his sadism a bit further by inviting his mother's best friend over. Saying that Clarnell wanted to see her, he convinced 59-year-old Sara Hallett to walk right into a vicious ambush. He leapt onto her, overwhelmed her with his huge bulk, and strangled her to death. After committing various outrages on her corpse, Kemper then cut Sara's head off, stuffed her in the closet, and affixed a note to her person. Directed to the police, it read, *Appx. 5:15 A.M. Saturday. No need for her to suffer any more at the hands of this horrible "murderous Butcher." It was quick—asleep—the way I wanted it. Not sloppy and incomplete, gents. Just a "lack of time." I got things to do!!!*

Kemper then took off on a nonstop drive to Colorado, fully expecting the police to be in hot pursuit. But after stopping over in Pueblo, Colorado, and tuning in to news stations on his car radio, he became convinced that no one was going to discover the grisly crime scene anytime soon. Deciding to take matters into his own hands, he went to a phone booth and dialed up the police himself to confess to his crimes.

Incredibly enough, they didn't believe him at first, even though they knew him and knew that he had killed his grandparents. It was only when he asked to speak to an officer that he was familiar with and fully explained the situation that he was taken seriously—and taken into custody. Kemper made a full confession to all of the murders he had committed, stood trial on November 8, 1973, and was found guilty as charged. He actually requested the death penalty, but the request was refused and he never did get to play "electric chair" for real. Instead he received a life sentence for each of his victims and was sent to the California Medical Facility, where he still languishes to this very day.

Archibald McCafferty
A Killer in Search of Seven Souls

Archibald McCafferty was a rare breed of killer. He didn't share many traits with other serial killers; he was not a loner, and although he had a criminal record for misdemeanors, he was not known to have any homicidal urges. But all that changed after a tragic accident killed his infant son. His wife had been breastfeeding the baby when she fell asleep and rolled over on top of him, smothering and killing him. This caused McCafferty to lose his mind. He completely snapped and sought revenge. But it goes deeper than that, because he actually heard the voice of his dead son telling him to kill seven people, which supposedly would somehow bring the baby back to life.

McCafferty committed his crimes in Australia, but he originally hailed from Scotland. His parents moved to Australia when he was 10 years old in search of a better life, but it seems that young Archie didn't find life better Down Under. He had a hard time adjusting to his new environment and released his angst by acting out aggressively. He was in and out of several institutions before he was 18.

When he met and married a woman named Janice, many hoped that settling down with her was just what McCafferty needed to start living the straight life. But problems were evident after just a few weeks of marriage, and McCafferty was soon caught in extramarital affairs. Then Janice discovered that she was pregnant with McCafferty's child. You might think that upon hearing such news this father-to-be would have reformed, or at least taken it easy on his new wife, but this was not the case. He routinely beat her and even choked her during the pregnancy. On one occasion he almost strangled her to death.

But when his son was born, McCafferty actually did change his ways. He seemed to truly love being a father, and it smoothed out some of his decidedly rough edges. The baby's arrival brought some much-needed happiness and stability into McCafferty's previously turbid life. So when Janice accidentally rolled over and killed the boy on March 17, 1973, the news was devastating not only to McCafferty but also to everyone who was hoping he had turned over a new leaf. They realized that the loss of the one thing that mattered to him could only result in a horrible downward spiral for McCafferty—and they were right.

The death was officially ruled an accident, but McCafferty did not agree. He quickly fired off an angry letter to the coroner charging that Janice had committed murder. McCafferty harbored nothing but hatred and rage toward his exonerated wife, and after a get-together with friends in the first week after his son's death, he attempted to corner her and attack her. Janice was expecting something like this might happen, though, and she was on her guard. She was able to slip away and ran off to another part of town where she could rely upon the protection of her brother. A crazed McCafferty tracked her down and came at her with a piece of picket fence, but he was grabbed by Janice's brother and his friend—who were apparently quite capable fighters—and given a thorough thrashing. Defeated and demoralized, McCafferty then turned up at his parents' home battered, bruised, bleeding and completely unhinged.

His mother pleaded for him to admit himself to a mental institution, and he was eventually escorted to the Parramatta Psychiatric Centre. However, he stayed there for just a few days before checking himself out. And the first place he went after he left was to the local tattoo parlor. McCafferty, you see, was a tattoo aficionado of the first order. He loved tattoos and his body was covered with them—so much so, in fact, that when he was eventually taken in on charges of murder, it took police several hours and several rolls of film to document the ink that covered him from head to toe. At the time of his discharge from Parramatta he only had one small spot left for a proper tattoo, just one patch of empty skin on his chest. He had been saving this for "something special", and after the death of his son, he suddenly had an idea of just what that was going to be. He had the number seven emblazoned right on the center of his chest— and would later claim that he heard the disembodied voice of his son telling him to do it and promising to come back to life if he struck down seven others.

As delusional as that may seem to anyone with a rational mind at their disposal, this was truly what Archibald McCafferty believed. After coming to this stunningly illogical revelation, McCafferty dropped out of sight for a while. Janice did not hear a word from him until about five months later when a brick sailed through her window. The brick had a note wrapped around it that read, *You and the rest of your family can go and get f—d, because anyone who has anything to do with me is going to die of a bad death. You know who this letter is from so take warning because Bill is the next cab off the rank. Then you go one by one.* This chilling threat was signed simply "You Know Who", but there could be no doubt that the author was Janice's estranged husband McCafferty—and it was also disturbingly clear that he was not going to let the accidental death of his son go.

Even while he was off the radar, McCafferty, a big fan of the movie *The Godfather*, was busy creating his own nefarious syndicate of mentally disturbed characters to help him exact his own warped vengeance. He had met two of the members of this outfit while doing time in the local psych ward. Their names were Carol Ellen Howes and Julie Ann Todd. Howes was a 26-year-old mother of three who was estranged from her husband. She was suicidal at the time, and it was McCafferty who had managed to talk her out of taking her own life. This apparently led to a strong friendship between the two, and shortly after their release they ended up moving in together. Todd, a mutual friend who was released at about the same time, simply had nowhere else to go, so she moved in too. The group was soon joined by Michael John Meredith and Richard Dick Whittington, shortly to be followed by Donald Richard Webster.

This gang of miscreants was cruising the streets in a stolen Volkswagen "looking for someone to beat up and rob" when they saw 50-year-old George Anson walking home from his shift. They made a beeline for Anson, closing in on him before he knew what was happening, and dragged him into an alley. At first they were only going to rob him, but then McCafferty heard a voice in his head reminding him to "Kill seven. Kill seven!" He obediently pulled out a knife and stabbed Anson several times. His acolytes, who hadn't heard any such voice, were thoroughly shocked, and Webster even dared to ask the question, "Why the f—k did you do that?"

McCafferty's only reply was to scream, "Drive, you f—g idiot!" His cowed crew silently obeyed his orders as he directed them to drive to a local fast food joint. The rest of the group ordered their burgers and fries—a macabre communion of youngsters now all complicit in a murder—while McCafferty went to the men's room to clean up. As he was washing his hands, he saw his son's face flash over his reflection and again heard the command "Kill seven". He stared in bewilderment as the image faded away.

And if this sounds strange, the testimony of this serial killer gets even stranger. Because just a few days later, on August 27th, while high on cocaine at his son's grave, McCafferty suddenly saw a bright light appear just overhead. He also saw a figure standing "just out of the light". It beckoned him to come forward, and when he did, the apparition asked, "Dad? Is that you, Dad?" Although McCafferty's son had died as an infant, his spirit had apparently returned as an older figure—at least old enough to speak.

Seeking to confirm this, McCafferty asked, "Is that you, Son?"

The ghost responded, "Yes, Dad, it's me."

Even the delusional, coked-up McCafferty saw a slight problem with this assertion. "But Son, it can't be. You're dead."

The figure then asked, "Do you want me to come back to you, Dad?"

"Of course I do," McCafferty gushed. "But how can you do that, Son?"

The spirit dodged the question and replied, "You've got to do something for me, Dad. Do this thing and I will come back to you. Do you want me to come back to you?"

Now, some have suggested that this apparition, far from being McCafferty's late son, was actually a demon leveraging his distress at the boy's death to get him to work evil in the world. And if that's the case, what McCafferty said next violated every rule in Demonology 101, because having been hit in the soft spot of his affection for his son, McCafferty responded wholeheartedly with, "Yes. Yes. More than anything in the world. I will do anything to have you back. Anything. Anything you ask."

It's never wise to tell the dark forces of eternal damnation that you will "do anything", and after McCafferty did just that, the spirit really let him have it and quoted him the price of his son's return as follows: "You must kill seven people. As soon as you do, you can have me back. But you must kill seven people. Kill seven. Kill seven. Kill seven."

Moments later, the spirit vanished, leaving McCafferty staring off into space in a state of shock—and just then a car pulled up containing two of his partners in crime, Todd and Meredith, along with 42-year-old Ronald Neil Cox as their newly captured hostage. Once again the crew's intent was to rob their victim, but McCafferty needed to slaughter another six souls for his son—as the voice in his head was constantly reminding him. So as the group forced Ronald out of the car at gunpoint and the poor man pleaded for mercy, McCafferty was not going to show one shred of compassion. Rationalizing to his comrades, "He's seen all of our faces—[we have to] kill him," McCafferty drew his own gun and prepared to open fire. Ronald desperately begged for his life on the grounds that he was the "father of seven children"—and as you can imagine, this didn't help matters much. When McCafferty's maddened mind heard the word "seven" he promptly emptied his pistol into the back of Ronald's head. McCafferty and his cohorts then hopped back in the car to flee the scene, and as they pulled out of the cemetery, he looked back just in time to see the light he had seen earlier remerge over his son's grave. A "shadowy figure" was standing within it, "laughing loudly" as if in triumph at the death of an innocent man.

The crew headed back to McCafferty's apartment to consume large amounts of beer and mindlessly watch television. But no matter how much McCafferty tried to drown it out, he still heard the voice of his son demanding that he kill a total of seven people as retribution for his untimely demise. So once again the group set out on their misanthropic mission. This time Todd and Whittington posing as hitchhikers to ensnare a helpful motorist named Evangelos Kolias. After they got inside his car, one of them pulled a gun and ordered him to lie down in the back seat, saying that if he complied, stayed quiet, and didn't give them trouble he would not be harmed.

This, of course, was a bold-faced lie since McCafferty still had five murder victims to go in his quest to kill seven. He intended to execute the vehicle's owner and then drive it to the family home of his estranged wife Janice, where he would kill her, her mother, and her mother's boyfriend—which would bring his tally up to a total of six. He told himself that his seventh and final target would be Webster, the one guy in his crew who had ever dared to question him.

Evangelos, who had been ordered to stay quiet in the back seat, had actually fallen asleep there by the time his kidnappers arrived at McCafferty's apartment—and he never woke up. McCafferty gave the order, and Whittington shot him twice in the back of the head. The group then dumped the body out of the car like a piece of refuse and drove on into the night in the stolen vehicle. The only thing that stopped them from driving straight to Janice's house was the fact that the car was about to run out of gas and none of them had any money to buy more.

McCafferty was forced to put off the planned attack for another day. But before he could get his gruesome action plan rolling again, fate intervened. Just as McCafferty had figured, he couldn't trust Webster, who had turned on him and informed the police about what was afoot. It was for this reason, and this reason only, that this serial killer's death toll would remain at three instead of the intended seven. (Upon his initial arrest, that is; the number would later rise to four when he killed a fellow inmate.)

But this was not the last strange twist in the story of Archibald McCafferty. Because incredibly enough, despite having received three consecutive life sentences, he was granted parole in 1993! The Australian government, though, was not prepared to be as lenient as the Australian courts and promptly deported him back to Scotland. Needless to say, the UK government wasn't exactly thrilled with this decision, but they had no choice but to accept the return of this wayward son of Scotland.

McCafferty moved back to his childhood stomping grounds and managed to stay off the radar for all of 18 months before being put on two years' probation for issuing threats to police officers. Is this the last we have heard off the unrepentant Archibald McCafferty? Is he still going to try to fulfill his pledge to sacrifice seven souls for his son? Only time will tell.

Dean Corll

The Candy Man

Dean Arnold Corll was one of America's worst serial killers. His killing spree during the 1970s was one of the most violent that the country had faced up to that point. His tendency to prey on children made his crimes all the more notorious. With deaths reaching almost thirty, it was perhaps the enlisting of two young accomplices that made people take note of the extreme manipulation and violence that was being carried out. Coupled with this, the lack of a true trial and punishment has led to there being a sense of unresolved justice about the case. But who exactly was Corll?

Growing up, Dean's father was very strict on the boy. But as the first born son, Dean was treated quite the opposite by his mother. She took an overbearing and overprotective approach to raising the child. This split between the ways the parents treated their son was reflected in other aspects of their relationship. Frequently quarrelling and often fighting, the parents – possibly inevitably – divorced in 1946. By this time, Dean was close to seven years old. Dean's mother, Mary, took the children and moved into a trailer in Memphis, Tennessee. The location was chosen so that the boys would have frequent chances to see their father, who had been drafted into the air force and was serving nearby. Following the breakup of the marriage, there would be a number of attempts to reconcile the relationship.

As a shy boy, Dean Corll had little contact with children his own age. Despite this, there have been numerous accounts that recall the ways in which he demonstrated great empathy and sympathy for others and attempted to help them. His childhood would be affected by illness when an undiagnosed bout of rheumatic fever led to the doctors discovering that Dean had a heart murmur.

Because of this, he was excluded from many of the more physical activities at his school.

Thankfully, 1950 would prove to be a more hopeful year for the family. Renewing their marriage, Dean's parents packed up the family and moved to Texas. This marriage would last only three years, however, and the couple again divorced. Following a fairly amicable divorce. Mary took custody of the children, and again she wanted them to be near their father. She would marry another man shortly after, a travelling clock salesman who encouraged the family to move to Vidor. This would be the place where Dean's family would open a candy store. Named "Pecan Prince," it started as a small experiment in their home before growing larger. For the young boys, they were given the task of operating the machinery for making the candy. This was then sold by their stepfather during his normal sales routes. They grew more popular than they might ever have imagined.

After a complicated childhood, Dean graduated with reasonable grades. Always regarded as something of a loner, he had intermittent relationships with a number of girls. It was noted that his only real hobby was the high school band, in which he played trombone. By the time he left school, the Corll family business was booming. The family relocated to larger premises outside of Houston to expand the business. Dean would spend two years away from Houston, moving to Indiana to care for his sick grandmother. When he returned to Houston, his mother's recent divorce made her form her own business, the Corll Candy Company. Dean was made vice-president. This was interrupted in 1964, when he was drafted for military service. Though he served for ten months without incident, he said later that he hated it. While in the military, he had his first encounters of a homosexual nature. The lasting effect, as he later told friends, was to help him realize that he was homosexual.

After being honorably discharged from the armed forces, Dean returned to his position as vice-president. The firm was running into stiff competition from Dean's former stepfather, and the two companies battled one another for market share. The Corll Candy Company moved to a bigger location in Houston to meet demand, opening a factory opposite an elementary school. Here, Dean was known to hand out free samples of candy to the local children. This practice would later lead to his nickname, the Candy Man. Some even took to calling him the Pied Piper. Reports seemed to indicate that Dean would occasionally flirt with the male employees of the company, though these advances were usually rebuffed. The company installed a pool table at the rear of the factory that became a popular gathering spot for young males.

In 1967, Dean would meet a twelve-year-old named David Brooks. David Brooks would play a key role in this story. Often hanging around boys older than he was, David would spend time in the Corll Company's pool room. He took the free candy from Dean, and the two struck up a bond. Along with numerous other teenage boys, Dean and David would take regular trips to the seaside. Dean provided David with money when he was lacking and became a kind of substitute version of a father figure in the young boy's life. From here, at the regular urging of Dean Corll, the two entered into a sexual relationship. For various sexual acts, Dean Corll would pay the young boy money. But the arrangement did not last. David's parents divorced, and he moved seventy-five miles away with his mother. On regular visits back to Houston, he would visit both his father and Dean. After a short while away, David dropped out of high school and moved back to Houston. By this time, he had come to regard Corll's home as his own.

The family business was not prospering, however. The Corll Candy Company closed in 1968, with Mary moving to Colorado.

Though she would speak with her son on the phone, they would never see one another again.

To make ends meet, Dean took on a job as an electrician. His crime wave would begin shortly after.

Dean Corll's crimes began in 1970. During a period of three years, he is thought to have killed at least twenty-eight victims and likely more. The majority of these victims were young boys aged between thirteen and twenty. He preyed on one particular area, Houston Heights, abducting boys from this location and taking them away. At the time, Houston Heights was not a prosperous area. To help him achieve his violent visions, Corll employed the help of two young boys; David Brooks and Elmer Henley. He would prey on the friends of his accomplices or set his sights on other boys whom he had spotted around town. He would get to know the victims before abducting them. Some of them were even former employees of the family business.

To better get away with his murders, Corll used a pair of vehicles. He owned both a Ford van and a Plymouth car, with a favorite trick being to offer a young boy a lift in either vehicle before simply driving away. Often, he would tempt his victims with drugs or alcohol, making them pass out or become dazed enough that he might be able to fit them with handcuffs. Others he would simply grab them using brute strength. Once he had them where he wanted them, Corll would strip his victims naked and tie them to either his bed or a specially constructed torture device that he had made from wooden boards. He would hang this device on the wall, leaving the boys manacled and unable to escape. Once trapped, Corll would begin a prolonged period of torture. This would involve them being beaten, sexually assaulted, and finally, killed. Sometimes they would be strangled to death, other times they would be shot with a small pistol.

Once deceased, they were wrapped in plastic sheeting and taken to one of four burial spots. These included a boat shed that Corll had rented, a distant beach, a wooded area near a family cabin he owned, and another beach near Jefferson County. In an attempt to distract distraught parents from tracking down their children, Corll would often try and forge messages from the boys. He might have them phone their parents or write a letter saying not to come looking. Every now and again, he would take a trophy from his victims. These were found after his death. At this time in his life, staying in one location seemed like a bad idea. As such, Dean Corll moved from town to town quite frequently but remained in and around the Houston area.

The first known murder committed by Dean Corll was an eighteen-year-old named Jeffrey Konen. Killed in September of 1970, he vanished while travelling with another student from the University of Texas to his parents' home in Houston. It is thought that Corll, who lived in the area, offered a lift to Konen, who accepted. The body would not be discovered for three years, not until David Brooks led police officers to the scene. It had been buried on a beach, and investigators were able to determine that Jeffrey had died of asphyxiation. The body was not just buried. It had been hidden beneath a large bolder, covered by a small amount of lime and wrapped in plastic. The body was naked and tied at the hands and feet.

Around the same time that Jeffrey Konen had been murdered, David Brooks discovered the extent of Corll's crimes. He walked in on Dean Corll in the act of torturing two boys whom he had strapped to a plywood board. Corll bought Brooks' silence. He offered him a car in exchange for remaining quiet. Brooks received a Chevrolet Corvette for remaining silent on the subject. After this, Corll offered him two hundred dollars for every boy who he could lure to the apartment. Brooks accepted.

The first time Brooks was involved in the murders was in December of 1970. Two boys – both mutual acquaintances of Brooks – were lured into Corll's apartment. Dean Corll tied them up, strapped them to his torture boards, raped, and strangled them. He buried the boys in a boat shed. Over the coming months, Brooks would be a participant in many more murders. They would all follow the same pattern, with Brooks helping Corll lure the unsuspecting boys into trouble before Corll tortured and killed them. In these cases, the parents would often launch huge searches for their missing boys. These would often involve poster campaigns to try and garner any additional information. One of the boys paid to hand out these fliers was named Wayne Henley, who was fifteen years old.

Elmer Wayne Henley was introduced to Dean Corll by David Brooks. While it is initially thought that he had been lured to the apartment as an intended victim, Corll saw something in the boy that changed his mind. He offered the same deal to Henley as he had to Brooks; two hundred dollars for every boy successfully tricked into the apartment. Corll informed the young Henley that he was part of a sexual slavery ring operating in the area. While Henley did not accept at first, the poor finances of his family led him to take up the offer in 1972. The luring of boys would follow a similar pattern, with both Brooks and Henley working in tandem to attract victims to Corll's home.

Over the next year, Corll began to kill more and more people. Fully aware of the fate of the boys that they lured to the apartment, Henley and Brooks continued to work for the serial killer. It is thought that there were deaths almost one a month around Houston, with Corll frequently moving and escaping detection. This would come to a head when he moved to a residence on Lamar Drive.

It was noted by both Brooks and Henley that Corll's move to this address prompted an upturn in the frequency and the brutality of the killings. At this point, both of the accomplices could tell when Corll felt in need of killing again. He would become agitated, would chain smoke, and would fritter and move chiefly on reflexes. At these times, he would tell them that he "needed to do a new boy." The attacks were only interspersed by a matter of days. This was despite the fact that David Brooks had taken a break from the crime spree to marry his pregnant girlfriend. The last victim, a boy of thirteen named James Dreymala, was abducted by both Brooks and Corll while on a bike ride. Like the others, he was strapped to the torture board, raped, and strangled to death before being buried.

***

Punishment would not arrive in the conventional form. While many serial killers are eventually caught and prosecuted to the fullest extent of the law, Dean Corll's downfall began like many of his killings. On the 7th of August, 1973, Henley began to work toward luring a nineteen-year-old boy named Timothy Kerley back to Dean Corll's apartment. Together, the pair drank and sniffed paint fumes. Brooks was not involved in this instance. The pair met up with a fifteen-year-old girl named Rhonda Williams, who was currently hiding to escape her abusive, drunken father. Henley invited them all to Corll's apartment, where they arrived at three in the morning.

Upon arrival, Corll was furious that Henley had bought "a girl" to his home. He informed Henley that this would ruin everything. Henley tried to placate Corll, and it appeared to work, with the host then offering the teenagers beer and drugs. They partook and began to party for the next two hours, at which point they passed out.

Henley awoke to find himself being tied up by Dean Corll. The murderer was still furious that he had invited Rhonda to the home and was taping his accomplice's hands and feet together. Already bound, the other teenagers were lying beside Henley. Kerley had already been stripped of his clothes. Noticing that his one-time accomplice was waking up, Corll came across to talk, removing the gag. He informed Henley of his anger at Rhonda's arrival and, as such, he was going to kill all three of them. While explaining this, he repeatedly kicked Rhonda in the chest. To demonstrate his seriousness, he picked up Henley and dragged him into the kitchen, where he placed a pistol to his chest.

Henley begged for his life. He promised to help kill the others. Corll finally agreed and went back into the main room. Here, he began to fasten Kerley to the torture board and demanded that Henley do the same to Rhonda. Handing his young accomplice a hunting knife, the killer told him to remove her clothes and get started. While Kerley writhed in agony, Rhonda turned to Henley and asked whether this was all real. After he had confirmed it as such, she simply asked him whether he was going to do anything about it.

Having second thoughts, Henley asked whether he could take Rhonda into another room. He was ignored. Henley reacted by grabbing the pistol and screaming at Corll, telling Corll that he had gone too far this time. Henley said he would not stand by any longer while all his friends were killed. Corll advanced on him. He told Henley to shoot him, daring him to pull the trigger. Henley backed off. Corll laughed and told Henley that he would never be able to do it. Henley pulled the trigger. He shot Dean Corll in the forehead, but the bullet bounced off the man's skull. Corll lurched forward, and Henley shot him again. And again. Hit in the shoulder, Corll stumbled out of the room, but Henley chased him and shot him as he walked down the stairs. Dean Corll died then and there, naked and covered in blood.

Henley ran back into the room and freed the teenagers. They debated what to do before Henley resolved to call the police. He phoned them and confessed to the shooting. At the station, when being questioned about just the death of Dean Corll, he admitted to his role in the other killings. After a period of disbelief, he offered to take the police to see the bodies. They travelled out to the boat shed, where many bodies were found in various states of decay. After being called in by the police, David Brooks also gave a full confession. The pair helped the police recover the bodies. At the time, it was the highest body count for an American serial killer.

While Dean Corll had died, both David Brooks and Elmer Wayne Henley were tried for their role in the deaths. Both men were found guilty and are serving life sentences for their roles in helping one of America's most violent, prolific, and sadistic mass murderers.

Paul John Knowles
The Casanova Killer

Paul John Knowles, sometimes known as the Casanova Killer, was born on April 17, 1946, in Orlando, Florida. His parents loved him like any other bundle of joy, and his childhood was fairly normal. But something changed when he hit adolescence. He began to commit petty crimes, and once he was caught and convicted, his authoritarian father washed his hands of him completely and sent him off to foster care. And as one might imagine, young Paul's behavior did not improve after this act of abandonment—it became worse.

So by the time Paul John Knowles became a serial killer in the summer of 1974, he already had a long rap sheet for lesser offenses. And in July of 1974, after getting arrested for getting into a bar fight, he turned his latest misdemeanor into a stepping stone for mass murder. He wasn't behind bars for long before he escaped by picking a lock and slipping out of jail unnoticed.

This underworld Houdini promptly went on a real rampage. First he burglarized the home of a 65-year-old woman named Alice Curtis. Knowles gagged Alice to keep her quiet while he stole her belongings, but she ended up suffocating, and the burglary turned into a murder. Undeterred, Knowles added grand theft auto to the growing list of charges when he fled the scene in Alice's car. Cruising the streets, he came upon two little girls named Mylette and Lillian. Fearing that they had witnessed his crime, he killed them and dumped their bodies.

Having gotten a taste for blood, he continued to kill random people all over rural northern Georgia. His next victim was Marjorie Howe, whom he strangled with her own stockings after breaking into her house and before taking off with her TV set. It seems a little unlikely that the money he got from pawning it was worth the trouble, but as senseless as his killings had been up to this point, they were about to get even more senseless.

His next victim was simply someone who was in the wrong place at the wrong time—a still-unidentified teenage runaway whom he decided to rape and kill for the mere "sport" of it. He carried out his next home invasion on August 23rd, when he broke into the home of Kathy Pierce. He throttled this young mother with a telephone cord, leaving her toddler as the only witness. Following this attack, Knowles lay low for the next couple of weeks, but he struck again on September 3rd after befriending a guy named William Bates at a bar in Ohio. Knowles used his charm to gain William's trust, and once his guard was down and they were away from prying eyes, this maniac choked his victim to death.

At this point, Knowles was killing just for the sake of killing. There was no rhyme or reason for it other than his own wish to kill. Nor was there any discernable pattern to his travels as he continued his murderous cross-country tour. From Ohio, he drove all the way to Texas in the car he had stolen from William Bates. He stopped when he caught sight of a woman in distress at the side of the road. She was apparently having car trouble and in need of assistance. Knowles, playing the Good Samaritan, volunteered to help this damsel in distress. But soon enough his inclination to help turned into an impulse to murder. He swiftly overpowered the woman and raped her before choking her to death.

But Knowles wasn't the kind of monstrous serial killer who could only get close to a woman through physical force. Later known as the Casanova Killer, Knowles was fully capable of turning on the charm if he wished. And when he met his next victim, Ann

Dawson, in Birmingham, California, he didn't have to use any coercion at all. He simply sweet-talked Ann so successfully that she became infatuated with the handsome stranger and willingly decided to go along with him on his journey. The Casanova Killer got bored easily, however, and after the fun had fizzled out a week later, he killed Ann and discarded her on the side of the road.

This crazed drifter then continued to roam the back roads of America looking for victims. Murder itself was now the primary motivation for Knowles, who had become addicted to the power he felt when he took someone's life with his bare hands. He only managed to abstain from spilling blood until October 19th, when he felt he had to have another "fix" to satiate his craving for homicide. He found it when he broke into 53-year-old Doris Hovey's house. It was a simple break-in, and upon confronting the homeowner he simply shot her execution-style and walked right back out.

Resuming his nefarious odyssey, Knowles picked up a couple of hitchhikers. He had marked them for murder, but before he could carry out the dread deed, he was stopped for a traffic violation. Knowles, even though he was still driving William Bates' car, took his chances and pulled over to the side of the road. If the police officer had taken the time to run the plates, he would have found that the car had been stolen from a murder victim and had more than enough reason to make an arrest—but as it was, he simply let Knowles off with a warning without even issuing a ticket. Nevertheless, that policeman can be credited with saving two lives that night, because Knowles was so shaken up that he couldn't bring himself to murder the hitchhikers. Instead, he drove them to their destination and bid them a courteous farewell, passing himself off as simply a kindhearted motorist helping a couple of strangers. Those two hitchhikers had just won the cosmic lottery, and they didn't even know it.

Still rattled and unsure of what to do next, Knowles drifted around until he made the acquaintance of one Carswell Carr. Always affable and always a conversationalist, Knowles wormed his way into Carswell's life to the point that he ended up hanging out at his house for a few drinks. But as the night wore on, Knowles suddenly turned on his new friend, pulled out a knife, and butchered him right on his own living room couch. Knowles then hunted down Carswell's 15-year-old daughter and choked her to death.

After this, Knowles resumed his regular routine of bar hopping across the country. On November 10th he ran into a woman named Sandy Fawkes. Sandy was drawn to Knowles' "gaunt good looks" and the two hit it off immediately. Sandy took Knowles home that night, and they ended up spending the next few days together. They parted company with Sandy still alive, but then Knowles returned to his fiendish form and cornered one of her friends, Susan Mackenzie. He pulled a gun on her and threatened to rape her, but she managed to escape and flag down a pair of policemen. The officers attempted to confront Knowles about the incident, but he likewise managed to get away.

Once he was sure the heat was off, he broke into the residence of Beverly Mabee in West Palm Beach, Florida. Although he left Beverly unharmed, he kidnapped her sister and stole her car. Strangely, Knowles decided to show mercy to his latest victim, even going out of his way to take her to Fort Pierce, Florida, where he dropped her off unharmed.

Of course, no good deed goes unpunished, and it was shortly afterward that a policeman finally recognized the stolen car and pulled Knowles over. Knowles got the drop on the officer, though, and holding him at gunpoint he managed to disarm him and take him hostage. Shoving the officer into the back of his own squad car, he got behind the wheel of the vehicle himself. A short time later, he used its siren to pull over a driver named James Meyer. Knowles tried to pretend that it was a normal traffic stop, but James soon realized that it was anything but. Knowles then pulled his gun and ordered James to get in the back seat with the captured cop. He drove the men to the woods, where he handcuffed them to a tree branch before shooting them both in the face.

The police were closing in, though, and soon enough Knowles became entangled in their dragnet. Approaching a police roadblock, he attempted to escape by crashing right through it, but his car careened to the side, spun out, and slammed into some nearby trees. Never willing to give up, Knowles hopped out of the smoking ruins of the car and took off on foot. Police officers and bloodhounds followed, it wasn't the police that took Knowles in that November 17th—it was an ordinary citizen hip to what was happening who managed to get the drop on Knowles, pull a gun on him, and order him to the ground until the police arrived.

Upon being taken into custody, Knowles readily admitted to killing 35 people. To this day, only 18 of those murders have been confirmed, but there was still more than enough evidence to schedule a trial. It never took place, however, because Knowles decided to make his final stand the very next day. He was being transferred from one facility to another, escorted by a sheriff and an FBI agent, when he suddenly reached for the sheriff's gun. That turned out to be the last thing he ever did, because the quick-thinking FBI agent Ron Angel immediately shot him dead for the infraction. For all of his suave, smooth machismo, it was all over in an instant for Paul John Knowles, one of the worst killers of the 1970s and in all of American history.

Kenneth Bianchi and Angelo Buono

Kenneth Bianchi was troubled from birth, born to a New York hooker and given up for adoption almost as soon as his mother checked out of the hospital. But despite this troubling beginning, Kenneth at first seemed to be one of the lucky ones, because he was soon scooped up by loving adoptive parents. Nicholas and Frances Bianchi both sought to pour all the care and affection they could into their adopted bundle of joy.

But Frances noticed that something was not quite right about her adopted son shortly after he stepped out of his playpen. As soon as the child started to talk, it became obvious that he was a pathological liar. He also had strange, trance-like daydreams. He was a smart kid, but also a chronic underachiever who never seemed to apply himself. Nicholas passed away in 1964, leaving a very worried Frances to raise Kenneth by herself.

Despite his problems, however, Kenneth Bianchi managed to graduate from high school in 1971. He wed his high school girlfriend shortly thereafter, but the marriage ended in divorce less than a year later when Bianchi's bride abruptly ran out on him without so much as an explanation. Bianchi then enrolled in college but failed to complete even his first semester. Disappointed and disillusioned, he bounced from dead-end job to dead-end job before eventually moving out to LA in 1977.

It was here that he reconnected with an older cousin of his named Angelo Buono, and this pair of angry young men soon formed a pact and developed a means to vent their rage— primarily upon unsuspecting young women. Bianchi and Buono concocted a plot to patrol the seedier side of the city pretending

57

that they were policemen. Their nefarious strategy was to flash fake badges at young women walking these troubled streets to convince them that they were undercover cops. They would then order the women into the back of their "unmarked police car".

This, of course, was just a ruse to get the women back to Bianchi's place so that they could take turns torturing and killing them. They would usually sexually assault the victims before strangling them, and it was this modus operandi that earned the pair the nickname of the Hillside Strangler.

Sickeningly enough, even while the cousins were brutalizing women by pretending to be police officers, Bianchi was actively applying to join the LAPD! Showing the true-blue colors of a sociopath, he was able to commit ruthless murders, then shrug them off and go hang out with a bunch of cops.

This ability to totally disconnect and dissociate from his crimes while living a completely different life as an aspiring LAPD trainee seemed to back up his later claims that he was suffering from multiple personality disorder. After his arrest, Bianchi asserted that he shared his head-space with a separate personality whom he called Steve Walker.

But whatever name he went by, Bianchi's days were numbered when in 1979 he lured two Western Washington University students into a building where he was working as a security guard and strangled them then and there. This was his first time to kill without Buono's help, and it showed. Unlike the previous ones, these murders were sloppy and left quite a bit of evidence behind—so much so that Bianchi was tracked down and arrested the very next day. His cousin went down shortly thereafter, and both were ultimately sentenced to life in prison, where they remain to this very day.

Juan Corona
The Grave Digger

One of most common ways attention is brought to the actions of a serial killer is thanks to the noise made by the victims' families. When a person goes missing, attempting to find them is the ultimate concern for those who are left behind. When the kidnapped have been taken by a serial killer, this process can lead to clues and answers being provided. But what will happen when the people who go missing have no one to search for them, no one to draw attention to their disappearance? In the case of Juan Corona, the missing people were those with few connections to the local area and very little in the way of people who might leap to their defense. Over a short period of time, this enabled Corona to kill at least twenty-five people.

Juan Corona was born in Mexico in 1934. Originally from a town named Autlán in the State of Jalisco, he crossed the border into the United States when he was just a teenager. Travelling to California, he made his money by working on American farms. He would work in Imperial Valley for a few months, gathering the crop of melons and carrots. He worked his way north, hoping to reach the Sacramento Valley. He knew that his brother had made a similar journey before him, leaving Mexico in 1944 and settling in Marysville. Juan joined him in 1953. At his brother's suggestion, he took up a job working on a nearby ranch. Shortly after, he met a woman named Gloria, and the pair got married. They would welcome four daughters into the world over the next few years.

In December of 1955, this area of California was hit by one of the worst floods in living memory. Throughout the history of California, there were few events that could match the destruction of the flood of 1955. Breaking through a levee in the west, a huge gush of water spread across an area as big as one hundred and fifty square miles. It left thirty-eight dead. Few could have predicted the effect that this event would have on Juan Corona. He suffered from an almost complete breakdown. Plagued by the flood, he became convinced that everyone he knew had actually drowned beneath the waters. Instead of living people, he believed anyone whom he encountered was actually a ghost.

This breakdown would later be diagnosed as schizophrenia. Noticing the fragile mental health of Juan, his brother had him taken away to DeWitt State Hospital, located in Auburn. He had Juan committed. Inside the hospital, the doctors were able to recognize Juan's ailments and decided that a course of shock therapy would be required in order to find a cure. Twenty-three times, Juan was treated using the now-outlawed electroshock treatment, in which a large electrical current is run through the temples. Declaring the patient to be cured, Juan was released to the outside world after just three months of being inside the hospital.

Following his release, Juan Corona was deported back to Mexico. He wanted to return to the United States and resolved to do so legally. To accomplish this, he applied for a green card. When his application was granted, he travelled back to his adopted homeland. Despite the occasional reoccurrence of the schizophrenic episodes, Juan gained a reputation as a hard worker. He had given up drinking but retained the violent temper that had stayed with him most of his life. His hard work paid off in 1962, when Juan Corona was hired as a licensed labor contractor. This required that he take control of the hiring of local workers to supply the ranches and farms in the area.

After years of being in close proximity with him, Juan's brother Natividad was beginning to notice issues his brother repeatedly demonstrated. Juan was careful to project an image of being a very macho person and often exhibited disputes with homosexual men. This was an issue for Natividad, who was gay and ran a café named the Guadalajara Cafe in Marysville. These concerns came to a head in 1970, when a patron of the café was attacked in the restroom by an unknown man wielding a machete. The young man, José Romero Raya, was discovered in the early hours of the morning, having suffered wounds to his face and head. Natividad called the authorities. Despite their inability to find the attacker, Raya sued the establishment and, by proxy, Natividad. After the courts sided with Raya and demanded that he be paid $250,000, Natividad decided that – rather than paying the amount – he would instead simply move back to Mexico. He sold his café and moved back home, leaving his brother behind.

Later that year, Juan was again committed to the same hospital where he had received electroshock treatment. Released a year later, he discovered that much of the ranch and farm work that he had relied upon had dried up. This led to him applying for welfare for the first time in 1971. Despite his lack of work, his assets (he owned two houses and had a small amount of savings) caused the application to be rejected. Around this time, police had begun to look into a number of disappearances connected to Juan Corona.

Without anyone realizing what had been happening, a number of migrant workers had been disappearing from the local area. Many were simply passing through, and some did not have the correct papers. Their disappearance often went unmentioned. People assumed they had simply wandered on to new pastures, but this was not the case. All of the vanished people had one thing in common; they had been known to work with Juan Corona. When their remains were discovered on the grounds of a number of ranches where Juan had worked, suspicions began to arise.

In particular, one of the graves bore a particularly damning piece of evidence. In the pocket of a corpse found in a shared shallow grave, the authorities found a receipt from a local meat store that held Corona's signature. Another pair of graves had bank slips which also featured that very same signature. As well as this, witnesses who were asked about the missing men often remarked that they had last seen them in the company of Juan Corona.

Throughout this time, Corona's actions had remained a mystery. While he had been killing these men, the manner in which he chose his victims meant that few people raised any surprises when they vanished. Due to the transient nature of migrant workers at the time, they were easy prey for a man like Juan. Thanks to his position of power, Juan was able to learn about the stories of these men and learn which ones would be the least likely to raise a fuss when they vanished. He abused this information and went on a killing spree. Once the victims were deceased, he would travel to the ranches and bury the bodies in shallow graves.

In May of 1971, the police believed they finally had enough evidence linking Corona to the killings. They obtained a search warrant, travelled to his home, and placed him under arrest. In the home, there was even more evidence. A pair of bloodstained knives were linked to the killings. There was both a machete and a pistol stored in the home, as well as several items of clothing that featured blood stains. Taking a work ledger from the premises, police were able to track down a number of names that tallied with those they knew to be missing and likely dead. Later, the prosecution team would come to refer to the names in this ledger as the "death list," indicating that it was the means by which Corona chose his victims.

***

Not a rich man, Juan Corona was provided with both legal aid and the help of a public defender. The first thing the lawyer did was to recruit a number of psychiatrists to perform an evaluation of the serial killer. A "not guilty" plea was entered in response to the authorities claims that they had found twenty-five bodies in the area, with the suspicion that there may have been many more. Corona hired a better lawyer. Rather than being able to pay him, however, he agreed that the lawyer would work for free in exchange for the rights to Corona's life. Should a book, television show, or film be made about Juan Corona's life, the lawyer would receive payment for the use of the story. The lawyer fired the previous psychology team, dismissed their reports, and advised that his client plead not guilty by reason of insanity. Before he could even get to trial, Corona suffered from a mild heart attack and was hospitalized on several occasions.

The trial took place in 1972 and took over three months to complete. After forty-five hours of deliberation, the jury returned a verdict of guilty on all twenty-five counts of murder. Each of these brought with it a life sentence. Housed in a medical facility due to the troubles with his heart, Corona was not entirely safe. On one occasion, he was stabbed over thirty times because he forgot to apologize after bumping into another inmate.

Eventually, a new trial was ordered. A new lawyer put forward the argument that the court had failed to take Corona's schizophrenia into account. During this second trial, the defense not only reminded everyone of Juan's mental health conditions, but they theorized that his brother Natividad could have been the potential murderer. They even suggested the attack on Romero Raya as being evidence of Natividad's prior violence. At this point, Natividad had been dead for eight years. Despite their best efforts, Juan Corona was again found guilty. To this day, he is still serving the sentences handed out by the courts. The authorities still do not have a firm number for the number of men he killed in California during the 1970s.

John Wayne Gacy
The Killer in Plain Sight

One of the most notorious serial killers of all time—John Wayne Gacy—had his reign of terror cut short as the 1970s were coming to a close. Gacy was a prominent member of Chicagoland social circles, frequently hobnobbing with politicians and hosting cookouts at his suburban home that were attended by many local VIPs. He was even in good with the Chicago PD—which served as a convenient shield for his less altruistic activities.

On one occasion, for example, a neighbor called the police to complain of screaming and "continuous shrieks" coming from Gacy's home. But when the cops came over, they just had a good-natured conversation with Gacy and informed the concerned caller that it was all just a false alarm—everything was fine.

Shortly thereafter, 15-year-old Robert Piest disappeared. Robert was a smart student who had a part-time job stocking shelves at a drugstore. On December 11, 1978, he informed his mother that immediately after work he would have an interview with a "building contractor" named John Wayne Gacy. When Robert never came home, law enforcement officials finally had to admit that their good pal Gacy was most likely up to no good. And when they ran a background check and found that he had been incarcerated about a decade prior for sexually assaulting another 15-year-old boy, they had no choice but to arrest him.

Searching his home, they found several pornographic magazines featuring young men having sex with older men, as well as a dildo smeared with feces as if it had been used anally. If nothing else, this was clear evidence that Gacy was living a double life. There was nothing illegal about that, of course, but as they continued to ransack Gacy's house, they uncovered several items that were clearly not his—articles of clothing and other accessories that would only have been worn by slim teenage boys, not an overweight man in his mid-30s like Gacy.

Considering that they had a missing 15-year-old boy whose last known whereabouts was Gacy's residence, this was more than a little alarming—but nowhere near as alarming as what they would find underneath a trapdoor that had been installed in the floor of a walk-in closet. This trapdoor opened up into the crawlspace beneath the house, and it was within this makeshift subterranean dungeon that the nightmare really began. The area was initially flooded, but after they had it drained, forensic specialists went down into a hidden world of horror. There were multiple bodies in various states of decay. Some were reduced to "lardlike globs" while others were mummies or skeletons. Only the most hardened of crime scene investigators were able to stomach the sight and smell of what they encountered long enough to document what would come to total 29 murder victims.

When confronted with this discovery, Gacy finally confessed to his crimes. He admitted to taking the boys to his home, sexually assaulting them, and then murdering them before callously dropping the corpses through the trapdoor. But even though he admitted to his deeds, Gacy attempted to circumvent justice by pleading insanity. Specifically, he claimed that "an evil alter ego named Jack" had coerced him into committing the murders. No one seemed to buy this excuse, though, and in March of 1980 Gacy was given a death sentence. After over a decade on death row, one of the worst serial killers of the 1970s breathed his last on May 10, 1994.

The world was waiting to see him die—and also waiting to see whether he would finally repent and apologize for his crimes when his last hour came. But those who were hoping for some contrition were sorely disappointed. Just minutes before his lethal injection, he was asked if he had any last words.

Gacy replied with a curt "Kiss my ass."

Richard Trenton Chase
A Former Mental Health Patient
Turned Serial Killer

One of the most important traits for those investigating the motivations and childhoods of serial killers is the presence of certain triggers and warning signs. Those who are labelled serial killers often share similar psychological tics which manifest in childhood and continue into their adult life. One man who exhibited such traits was Richard Chase, otherwise known as the Vampire of Sacramento. Born in California, Chase's childhood was not a happy one. Beaten by his mother, he was known to exhibit what is now known as the Macdonald Triad. These are enuresis (a repeated inability to control urination), pyromania (an inability to fail to resist impulses to deliberately start fires), and zoosadism (pleasure derived from cruelty to animals).

As he grew into adulthood, he became dependent on alcohol and developed hypochondria. Chief among his complaints was a belief that his heart would frequently stop beating or the insistence that someone had taken away his pulmonary artery. He shaved his head in the belief that he could watch his skull shifting beneath the skin and believed he could absorb the vitamins of an orange through the palm of his hand.

He left home and moved in with friends. These people came to resent his frequent use of psychedelic drugs and reliance on drinking. Chase would also make his roommates uncomfortable by strutting around the house without clothes. After he refused to move out, everyone else left. At this point, Chase began to trap and kill animals in the home, often disemboweling his prey and eating their flesh raw. This, he suggested, stopped his heart from shrinking. In 1975, he was committed to a mental health ward.

He told staff about his various fantasies about killing rabbits and even managed to capture, kill, and eat birds inside the facility. Over time, he developed the nickname "Dracula."

During his stay, he claimed to have drained blood from a therapy dog and frequently defecated in the ward, smearing his feces around the walls. This behavior eventually led to a diagnosis of paranoid schizophrenia. With a prescribed list of medicines, Chase was released into the care of his mother. Over the coming years, she began to ease her son off the medication and eventually found him an apartment. In the summer of 1977, Chase was stopped by the police. He was smeared with blood and had a bucket of even more blood in his truck. This was later found to be cow's blood, and he was released once again.

The first known murder at the hands of Richard Chase occurred on December 29, 1977. Ambrose Griffin was a father in his early fifties, shot down by a driver who sped away. Police investigated the local area but found no leads. After two weeks, Chase then attempted to gain entry to a locked home. Failing to get through the lock, he would later mention that locked doors were a signal of him not being welcome in a home. He was chased from one home after defecating on the bed and clothes of a couple. They chased him from their house, but he remained at large.

The next victim was a women named Teresa Wallin. A pregnant woman, Chase shot her three times while she was at at home. He then proceeded to rape the corpse, using a butcher knife to stab her during the act. Before he left, Chase took several organs, a nipple, and drank some of her blood. His final act was to remove dog feces from the lawn and to jam them down his victim's throat.

The final murders committed came at the end of January. Evelyn Miroth was entertaining Danny Meredith at her home when

Chase entered. He shot them with his handgun and moved through the home, stealing wallets and car keys. Also in the house were Evelyn's son and nephew, aged six years and twenty two months respectively. He shot them both. As with Teresa Wallin, Chase engaged in sex acts with the body of the woman he had just killed. He was disturbed from this when there was a knock at the door. Evelyn's son was expecting a play date with a local six-year-old girl. She was at the door. Chase ran, taking the son's body with him. Finding no one home, the girl alerted a neighbor, and the police were called. When they walked into the home, they found Chase's bloodied handprints around the home. He was quickly tracked down.

After being caught, Richard Chase was tried for six murders. In an attempt to avoid execution, Chase's lawyers suggested that his actions were second degree murders, a charge carrying a life sentence. With Chase's history of mental health issues, they felt his crimes were not of a premeditated nature.

The case received a huge amount of attention. On May 8, the jury returned a verdict of guilty on all counts of first degree murder. Chase would face the gas chamber. In jail, Chase's reputation preceded him. Other inmates were wary of their murdering cellmate. According to those working at the jail, some criminals imprisoned with him tried to convince Chase to kill himself.

The story does not end there. Chase allowed a reporter, Robert Ressler, to conduct a number of interviews. During these sessions, Chase shared his fears of alien invasions and Nazis. The murders, he suggested, were not his fault. Instead, they were acts of self-preservation, essential for him to continue living. He requested Ressler obtain a radar gun on his behalf, to better fight the Nazi aliens, and handed the interviewer a large amount of pasta and cheese which he had been keeping in his pocket. He suspected the guards were in league with his extra-terrestrial tormentors and were trying to kill him.

The day after Christmas, 1980, a guard checked in on Chase's cell. He was found lying awkwardly and was not breathing. He had committed suicide, with autopsy reports indicating he had been stockpiling prescribed anti-depressants in order to purposefully overdose. Despite his spree only lasting a month, Chase's position in the media and his recorded interviews gave the public a real insight into the mind of a serial killer.

Charles Sobhraj
The Tourist Killer

While many serial killers strike out at unassuming victims under the cover of darkness and mystery, some reach out from under the cover of friendship. Chales Sobhraj was a killer who earned the trust of travelers and preyed on a belief in the kindness of strangers. He was born in Saigon, the son of a Vietnamese mother and an Indian father who were not married. His father would later leave the family to fend for themselves. After his mother met a new boyfriend, Sobhraj was adopted by the French Army lieutenant with whom his mother had fallen in love. After the couple had children of their own, Charles would find his parental affections sidelined. The family moved back and forth between France and South East Asia, and Charles began to develop an interest in petty and minor crimes.

This interest would result in a first jail sentence after being caught committing burglary in 1963. He served his time in a Parisian jail, using his charm to convince the guards to permit him special privileges. Unlike other prisoners, he was allowed to keep books in his cell. One man who volunteered at the prison was Felix d'Escogne, a wealthy individual with whom Sobhraj struck up a friendship. After being released, he would move in with Felix, splitting his interests between the criminal underworld and the bourgeoisie Parisian upper classes. Using a series of thefts and scams, he built up a small fortune of his own. It was during this time he met Chantal Compagnon, the daughter of a conservative family. On the day he asked for her hand in marriage, Sobhraj was arrested for being the driver of a stolen vehicle. He served eight months in jail. The couple married when he was once again a free man.

Together, they travelled to French controlled areas of Asia to avoid the attentions of the law. They would use falsified documents and would rob tourists who they began to befriend. Finally, in 1970, they arrived in Mumbai with their daughter, Usha. Sobhraj turned back to a life of crime. He organized a vehicle stealing operation, smuggling the cars in and out of the country. Rather than spending his profits on his family, he developed an addiction to gambling.

After attempting to rob a jewelry store in 1970, Sobhraj was arrested. He escaped by enlisting his wife's help in feigning an illness. Despite getting free, they were soon recaptured, and Sobhraj was forced to borrow money from his father to pay his bail. The family took flight and journeyed to Kabul.

Here, they began their business of robbing visitors to what became known as "the hippie trail." They befriended foreigners, offered guidance, and then took their belongings. He was once again arrested and used the same illness trick to escape. This time, when fleeing to Iran, Sobhraj did not bring his family. Chantal was beginning to have doubts about their life style, and she returned to France with their daughter. Over the next two years, Sobhraj attempted to evade the law. With nearly a dozen stolen passports, he moved through Eastern Europe and the Middle East. He connected with his younger brother, Andre when he reached Instanbul, when the two quickly struck up a criminal relationship. Andre was captured in Greece. Charles escaped but was forced to leave his brother behind to serve an eighteen-year sentence.

The real crimes would begin now, as Sobhraj began to pose as either a drug dealer or a gem expert, working his magic on tourists as they travelled across Asia. Once ingratiated, he would rob his new friends and run. During this time, he began to build up a cadre of devoted followers, people who trusted Sobhraj completely and were content to do his bidding.

He would often arrange for difficult situations for travelers to enter into. Missing passports was a familiar scheme, with tourists scared of how they might recover their lost documents. In reality, they had already been stolen, but Sobhraj would befriend and help the victims before robbing them of even more money. He might suggest that a tourist had contracted dysentery when, in fact, they had been poisoned at his hand. A young Indian man named Ajay Chowdhury would become the second in command of Sobhraj's expanding criminal crew.

The first murders were committed in 1975. Later police investigations revealed the first victims to be members of the crew who threatened to reveal Sobhraj's crimes to the authorities. The girl – Teresa Knowlton from Seattle – was discovered, her body floating in a pool near the Thai coast. She had been drowned. First thought to be an accident, a later autopsy revealed the true nature of her death months later. The next victim was Vitalli Hakim, whose burned body was found near the gang's hiding place in Pattaya.

One example of the gang's murderous modus operandi was the case of Henk Bintanja and Cornelia Hemker, a betrothed Dutch couple in their late twenties. They met Sobhraj in Hong Kong and were convinced to travel with him to Thailand. There, they were poisoned and nursed back to health by the crew. This act gained their trust, with everyone telling them they had contracted an illness. Worried about attracting attention, the couple were strangled, their bodies burned and dumped near the gang's hideout. The gang then took the pair's passports and used them to travel to Nepal.

This process continued, meeting tourists, befriending them, killing them, and stealing their wealth and travelling documents. Once the act of murder had been committed, Sobhraj and his gang would move to the next country before the bodies could be identified. The gang followed Sobhraj across countries and continents, including visits to Calcutta, Bangkok, and Nepal. Difficulties in tracking the fake names and a lack of collusion between police meant the scope of their actions was not realized. In the West, countries such as the Netherlands and France began to investigate reports of teenagers disappearing during their travels. There were even instances of governments covering up the murders, with countries such as Thailand fearing that the reveal of the murders would lead to a fall in the tourism industry.

Leading the investigation in Holland was a diplomat named Herman Knippenberg. He had become aware of Sobhraj's criminal activities. It is reported that he may even have met the man, though Sobhraj's name was still unknown at this point. Using the evidence he gathered with the help of a neighbor, Knippenberg was granted a search warrant for Sobhraj's apartment. Inside, he found stolen documents and passports, in addition to poisons and medical equipment.

Meanwhile, Sobhraj's gang of three was travelling through Malaysia. At this point, Chowdury went missing, with witnesses recalling him giving Sobhraj a large number of jewels. Now working with just one partner, Sobhraj travelled to Geneva and posed as a gem salesman. Though his death had been unconfirmed, no trace of Chowdury was ever been substantiated. With the proceeds from this sale, Sobhraj began to recruit members for his gang. During this time, their actions brought about the death of Luc Solomon, a Frenchman the gang poisoned. Designed to incapacitate him and build trust, the poison instead took his life.

Sobhraj was captured in New Delhi in 1976. Having convinced a group of French students to let him be their tour guide, he provided them with what he described as anti-dysentery tablets. When the poison began to act quicker than anticipated, several of the students fell unconscious. Realizing what was happening, those still awake attacked Sobhraj and detained him. They handed him over to the authorities with a description of his crimes. Police also began to question the members of his gang. While Sobhraj held out, his newly recruited accomplices quickly cracked. They confessed to the murders. Sobhraj was charged and sent to prison in Tihar as he awaited the beginning of his trial.

Inside the jail, conditions were so tough as to drive two of the gang into attempting suicide. They would remain in this jail for two years as the trial was put together. Unlike his fellow criminals, however, Sobhraj had been in possession of many gems when entering the jail. Using these, he bought and bartered for special privileges, turning his incarceration into a more pleasant experience.

When the trial started, Sobhraj exhibited his flair for showmanship. Attracting media attention, he would fire and hire lawyers frequently, even recruiting his newly released brother Andre as part of the legal team. He starved himself, telling people he was hunger striking. Despite this, he was sentenced to jail for a period of twelve years. With many predicting the death penalty, it was thought Sobhraj had gotten off lightly.

Inside the jail, Sobhraj began to exert his influence and bribed many of the guards. Leading a "life of luxury," his television and gourmet meals were a result of a friendship with both guards and prisoners. He began to spread his fame worldwide, encouraging Western authors and journalists to write about his life. He discussed his murders freely, describing events without ever actually admitting to his own involvement. His motives, he began to suggest, were to avenge the history of Western imperialism in Asia.

Despite his incarceration in India, Sobhraj was still a wanted man. An arrest warrant in Thailand would mean being tried for crimes punishable by death. On the tenth anniversary of his time in jail, he used his influence to throw a huge party for the guards and the prisoners alike. Here, he poisoned all in attendance and simply walked out of the jail. He was arrested in Goa while eating at a restaurant and was sentenced to a further ten years. This had been his plan all the long. By the time he was finally released again, the warrant for his arrest had expired, witnesses had disappeared, and evidence had been lost. With no outstanding criminal charges, he was allowed to return to France.

Returning to Paris, Sobhraj began to revel in his own notoriety. He recruited a publicity agent to spread his fame and charged the press for access to his story. It is thought that he accrued close to fifteen million dollars in this manner by selling the rights to a film based on his story.

In 2003, he returned to Nepal for unknown reasons. Here, he was captured and thrown in jail. Quickly, Sobhraj moved to have the case squashed and complained about his lack of a fair trial. In France, his estranged wife Chantal was said to be submitting a case to the European Court of Human Rights, due to the fact that the French government refused to provide assistance. In 2005, his conviction was deemed to be legitimate. After being at the center of three documentary films and four books, some have suggested that Charles Sobhraj was desperate for attention and returned to Nepal to increase interest in his own notoriety. He resides in jail to this day, found guilty of a number of murders.

As he still protests his innocence, we may never know the true extent of his prolific killing spree.

Peter Sutcliffe
The Hammer and Knife Killer

Many experts trace the modern concept of the serial killer back to the crimes of the man known as Jack the Ripper in Victorian England. As one of the lasting legacies of these crimes, the suffix "ripper" has been used to describe a number of modern killers. One of the most infamous is Peter Sutcliffe, the man who came to be known in the press as the Yorkshire Ripper.

Sutcliffe – as his alias suggests – was a native of the north English town of Yorkshire. He came from a working class background, born into a family who were strongly linked to the Catholic faith. As a noted loner and isolated figure during his childhood, he left school at the age of fifteen without feeling the need to pursue his education. In the working world, he began to search for a job, taking on a number of menial positions at this time. One of the most memorable was his time as a gravedigger in the 1960s. He worked in the packing department of a television company, and then, when asked to become a travelling salesman for the same company, he left.

After this, he took time off from his temporary night job to earn his truck driving license. His first position in this industry – delivering tires for a local company – resulted in him being dismissed for suspected theft. He variously held a number of positions as a truck driver throughout the 1970s, during which time it is suspected he began soliciting prostitutes. One of the formative experiences attributed to him by experts is the possible losing of a large amount of money to one such sex worker.

In 1974, he married his girlfriend, Sonia Szurma. They had met seven years previously and, after several attempts to conceive a child, they discovered that Sonia was unable to become a mother. Instead, she resumed her training to become a teacher and entered into an affair with an ice cream seller. Sutcliffe remained unaware. The two bought a house using Sonia's earnings as a teacher. They would still be living in this home when Sutcliffe was later arrested.

Doctors and experts who examined Sutcliffe's early life have stated that they were unable to find anything distinctly abnormal during his childhood. However, his early adulthood – and in particular his time working digging graves – had an adverse effect on his personality. During this time, he began to build a reputations as a dark and macabre person, noted for his twisted humor. He is also noted for his voyeuristic attitudes and his repeated spying on prostitutes and various sex workers from a distance.

It is widely regarded that Sutcliffe's history as a serial killer began in 1969. His first act was to assault an older prostitute. Searching for the money he believed he had been scammed out of, he travelled with a friend to search for the woman. During his search, he vanished up a road, out of sight of his friend. Upon his return, he was noticeably out of breath and instructed his friend to drive away quickly. According to Sutcliffe, he followed the woman into a garage and hit her over the head with a rock stowed inside a sock. In his own words, the force of the blow was enough to tear the toe of the sock, sending the stone flying across the room. The assaulted woman noted the license plate of the vehicle in which they escaped and called the police. To the police, Sutcliffe said he had used his hand to hit the woman. The woman, according to the police, was unwilling to press further charges and wanted nothing more to do with the incident. The police left Sutcliffe alone.

The second violent incident came several years later, in the summer of 1975. Anna Rogulskyj was walking by herself when attacked. This was the first instance of Sutcliffe using the weapon he would come to be associated with: a ball-peen hammer. As well as hitting her over the head, Sutcliffe used a knife to slash open her stomach. The attack was interrupted by a neighbor, and Rogulskyj survived. A medical procedure managed to save her life, but she was left traumatized by the attack.

The Yorkshire Ripper's next victim was Olive Smelt. Sutcliffe attacked in the same manner, using the combination of a hammer and a knife to take down his victim from behind. Once again, Sutcliffe was interrupted, and Smelt was left alive but traumatized. The same month, fourteen-year-old Tracy Browne was attacked, again with the hammer. After being disturbed during the attack by the lights of a passing car, Sutcliffe left Browne where she lay. She would survive but would need brain surgery.

The first woman Sutcliffe killed was Wilma McCann. A mother of four, Wilma died on October 30. She was struck twice over the head before being slashed with the knife fifteen times. Investigators would find traces of semen on her clothes. Her death would alert the police to the seriousness of the crimes being committed.

It would be four months before Sutcliffe's next murder. Emily Jackson was stabbed fifty-one times by Sutcliffe. Having fallen on dire financial times, Jackson had begun to solicit sexual clients using a family-owned van. Once Sutcliffe had hit her over the head with his hammer, he sharpened a screwdriver to a point. He drove it into her neck, her abdomen, and her chest. Finally, he stomped on Jackson's thigh and left behind the imprint of his boot.

The third killing of 1976 would be Marcella Claxton, who was attacked while walking home from a party on May 9. Needing to urinate, she left her car on the side of the road. Sutcliffe came from behind and hit her with his hammer. Although she was left wounded on the side of the road, Claxton survived. She would be one of the witnesses who would testify at Sutcliffe's trial.

The following February, a prostitute named Irene Richardson was attacked in Roundhay Park. Another victim who was hit over the head with the hammer, Richardson would be one of the bodies with whom Sutcliffe interfered following her death. He used his knife to mutilate her corpse but again left behind a clue for investigators. The tire marks of his vehicle were readily identifiable at the scene of the crime.

The next murder was Patricia Atkinson. On April 23, she was killed in her flat, and once again, Sutcliffe left behind a print of his boot, this time on Atkinson's bed sheets. Jayne MacDonald, just sixteen at the time of the attack, was killed two months later. The fact that she was not a sex worker opened the public's eyes to the potential threat the Yorkshire Ripper posed to all women, regardless of their profession.

Maureen Long was attacked in July but survived. Sutcliffe attempted to murder Long but was interrupted and forced to flee. Witnesses described what they saw to the police but incorrectly identified the car Sutcliffe was driving. By this point, over three hundred policemen had been drafted into the investigation. Though thousands of car registrations were checked, but nothing was found since the investigations were built on incorrect accounts. On October 1, Jean Jordan was killed by Sutcliffe, but her body was not found for ten days. It appeared that the body had been moved several days after the murder, as Sutcliffe had realized a bank note he had passed to the victim would be traceable. When arriving back at the body, Sutcliffe could not find the note and instead mutilated the corpse and moved it to another location.

Jordan's body would be discovered the morning after it had been moved. She had been hidden near an allotment garden and was found by a dairy worker tending to his own plants. The traceable note was stashed away in a hidden compartment of Jordan's handbag, and its discovery would play a key role in tracking down the killer. Thanks to the particular note, police were able to trace the location to a specific branch. Police analysis of bank operations allowed them to narrow their field of inquiry to eight thousand employees who could have received it in their wage packet. They followed this up by interviewing thousands of employers who might have included the note in an employee's pay packet. Over three months, the police interviewed five thousand men, including Sutcliffe. During his interview, the alibi Sutcliffe provided was deemed to be credible. The party he had attended was one he later left in order to commit the crimes, but those at the party were able to confirm his attendance. This meant the vital clue found by investigators had led nowhere.

The final attack of 1977 was Marilyn Moore, a sex worker from Leeds. She lived and was able to provide the police with a description of the man who attacked her. As well as this, tire imprints from the crime scene matched those found at an earlier attack.

In 1978, Sutcliffe killed three women. His final attack of the year came in May, after which it was almost a year before he struck again. During this time, Sutcliffe was dealing with the death of his mother. His next victim was Josephine Whitaker, who was attacked on April 4, 1979. She was a clerk for a building society and had been walking home from work. The police had become distracted by a recording sent to their headquarters purporting to be by the Ripper. Based on the accent, investigators tracked their suspect down to a specific area of Sunderland. The messages were, however, a hoax. John Humble would later be convicted for attempting to pervert the course of justice.

Sutcliffe's next victim was Barbara Leach, a local student. She was the sixteenth victim. Her body was placed beneath a pile of bricks near her university. At this point – even in spite of the red herring voice messages – Sutcliffe was interviewed by police on two more occasions. This count would eventually reach nine, and even though he had been placed on a shortlist of three hundred suspects, he was not among the highest ranking in police thoughts.

In April of 1980, Peter Sutcliffe was caught driving under the influence of alcohol. While he awaited trial for this crime, two more women were killed. Sutcliffe also attacked three further women who managed to survive. On November 25, a known associate of Sutcliffe named Trevor Birdsall reported his friend as a possible suspect. This was added to a pile of ever mounting paperwork.

Sutcliffe was caught on January 2, 1981. Stopped by police, he was in the company of a prostitute named Olivia Reivers. The police checked the vehicle and found it to be fitted with false license plates. Sutcliffe was arrested. Police questioned him in connection with the Ripper murders and noted his likeness to physical descriptions of the killer. The next day, they discovered a hammer, a knife, and a rope that had been stashed in the car during his arrest. A second knife had been hidden in the cistern of a police toilet during his time in custody. They wrote a search warrant for his home and began to question his wife.

Police inspected Sutcliffe's clothes and found him to be wearing a specially fitted pullover beneath his trousers, the neck hole designed to provide access to his genitals during an attack. Padding around his knees had been added and would allow him to crouch down over his victims. This information and the sexual implications it contained were not revealed to the public until 2003. Police interrogated Sutcliffe for forty-eight hours until, quite suddenly, he confessed to being the Yorkshire Ripper. Once this admission was made, he proceeded to describe in detail many of his attacks. After several weeks, he declared God had told him to commit the murders. Of all the accounts, only the story of Jayne MacDonald (his youngest victim) brought forth an emotional response.

At trial, Sutcliffe entered a not guilty to thirteen murder charges. He instead asked for a charge of manslaughter based on reasons of insanity, referencing the will of God in his attacks. He suggested that he had begun to hear voices while digging graves, voices that had ordered him to murder sex workers. Of all the graves, it was the grave of Bronisław Zapolski that Sutcliffe suggested made the demands. He also pleaded guilty to the attempted murder of seven women. His diminished responsibility plea was rejected, and the trial lasted two weeks. Peter Sutcliffe was found guilty of thirteen murders and sentenced to life in jail. He remains in prison to this day. During his incarceration, he has been at the center of four different attempts on his life, losing an eye during one attack. Politicians have constantly reiterated that it is unlikely he will ever be viable for parole.

Don't Panic at the Disco

The 1970s were a time of fun and fashion, freedom and revolution—especially within the youth culture of the United States. But along with all the disco raves and idle days spent smoking sinsemilla, there was a dark shadow that permeated the soles of even the sturdiest of platform shoes. In many ways, the 1970s was as a breath of fresh air after the continuous ideological struggles of the 1960s. But there was something else in the air besides the music of KC and the Sunshine Band— there was a real undercurrent of mayhem perpetuated by some of the worst serial killers ever known to man.

In this book we have explored some of the darkest depths to which these outlaws of society dragged their fellow humans down. Many then, when they saw the horrific news reports detailing the atrocities committed by these butchers, were tempted to just change the channel; and many of us now are no doubt tempted to just forget all about them. But ignoring these misanthropic works of man is not going to do anyone any good. Changing the channel is not going to change the minds of those who are hopelessly warped and bent. Instead of panicking at the disco and hiding these real-life monsters in the dark, bring them right out into the light. Because just as your mother told you when you feared the bogeyman in the closet, the best way to chase away these nightmares is always going to be—to face them.

Further Readings

Here in this chapter we would like to present some of the reading and reference materials that helped to make this book possible. They may seem a little wide-ranging, but rest assured that they all go back to the main theme of serial killers of the 1970s.

The Serial Killer Files. Harold Schechter

This book houses a wide-ranging anthology of just about every serial killer you could ever think of, so although it doesn't specifically focus on the 1970s it contains quite a few cases from that decade. Mr. Schechter's reporting is to the point, straightforward, and unbiased. If you need information on any of the cases presented here, this book is a good place to start.

My Life among the Serial Killers.
Helen Morrison & Harold Goldenberg

This book provides some great insights into the personal lives and motivations of a wide variety of serial killers. If you need a book that focuses on the warped psyches of mass murderers, this one provides a tremendous window into the dark machinations of these madmen's minds.

Also by Jack Smith

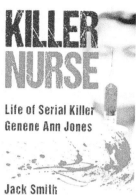

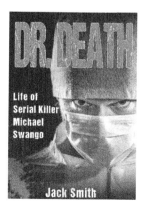

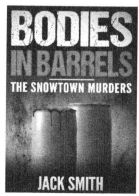

Printed in Great Britain
by Amazon

79991203R00058